PRAYER FOR
BEGINNERS

Prayer for Beginners

JOHN RYELAND

Foreword by Richard Harries,
Dean of King's College, London

MOWBRAY
LONDON & OXFORD

Copyright © John Ryeland 1985

ISBN 0 264 67038 8

First published 1985
by A.R. Mowbray & Co. Ltd,
Saint Thomas House, Becket Street,
Oxford, OX1 1SJ

Typeset by HiTech Typesetters Ltd, Oxford
Printed in Great Britain by Richard Clay
(The Chaucer Press) Ltd, Bungay, Suffolk

British Library Cataloguing in Publication Data
Ryeland, John
    Prayer for beginners.——(Mowbray's popular
    Christian paperbacks)
    1. Prayer
    I. Title
    248.3′2   BV215

    ISBN 0-264-67038-8

To my wife
GILLIAN

Contents

Foreword

Someone I knew once described himself to me as 'an emergency Christian', meaning that he only prayed when things got bad. Then, with an endearing honesty, he admitted that he seemed to have 'an awful lot of emergencies'. There is nothing to be ashamed of in praying when we are in difficulties. Indeed we should pray at all such times. For God is there to help us and calling upon him in times of trouble deepens our proper dependence on him. But how do we enlarge the scope of our prayers so that it consists of more than asking God for things? John Ryeland's book is written for people who feel that they are starting at the beginning. It assumes nothing. It is written in a straightforward, untechnical style. It is friendly, conversational and designed to be a help. In this it admirably succeeds.

In addition to those wanting to pray seriously for the first time, this book is designed for people whose prayer has become repetitive and dull. The book is full of useful suggestions on how our prayer can be refreshed, from turning breathing into an act of prayer to making a service on the radio or TV a true act of worship. It offers advice on meditation, the use of silence and many other aspects of prayer. There is something useful here for everyone.

One strength of this book is that it never forgets that prayer is about sustaining and deepening a relationship. These are not techniques to achieve a particular state of mind but expressions of a relationship with God established through Jesus Christ. Prayer is not an optional extra for this relationship. It is at its heart; it is this relationship. As Peter Baelz has put it 'To cease to pray would be to cease to believe'. This book offers practical, down-to-earth advice on how to pray and through praying, on how to believe with greater depth and reality.

Richard Harries
Dean of King's College, London

Introduction

As a priest I come across many people who regularly attend church and give generously of their time and money in helping the life of the church, whether it be through dutiful attendance, or serving on the flower rota, singing in the choir, or sitting on committees. Yet despite this commitment many people have a very real difficulty when it comes to saying their daily prayers. It may be because they are young or just approaching confirmation and have never been taught what it is to pray, and what prayer means. In their Confirmation classes they may learn much about the Church and the central beliefs of the Christian faith, but often, even after these classes, they have drawn no closer to God through the practice of prayer. Many other committed churchgoers find prayer difficult because of the lack of time available to them, and so prayer and the reading of the Bible get squeezed out of their daily lives and relegated to Sunday worship. Still others are able to make the time and know the necessity of prayer in their lives, but they do not know what to say in their prayers or how to express their deepest longing in prayer or even if they should voice such longings at all.

Nobody finds prayer easy, and if an expert is someone who has mastered a particular field, then there are few experts in prayer. Every Christian who has ever prayed will have experienced something of the frustration of crying out to a God who does not seem to be present, with words that do not seem to voice themselves. At times the more that there is to pray about, the worse this feeling can seem.

Talking to God is difficult, for God is a very different being from man; often our wills do not coincide and our minds do not seem to meet. It requires determination to spend time, effort and imagination in building up a relationship with God, just as it does in building up relationships with other people. This is what prayer is about.

Personally I have never found it that easy to sit down and pray. I have always found it helpful to have at my disposal certain 'schemes', practical aids and patterns of prayer on which to hang my own prayers. This is what this book is about. It is an attempt to pass on to others some of the methods of prayer used by many different people. It should be said at this point that none of these methods are *the* way of praying; many people have their own outlines and methods, and if these 'work' then that is marvellous. I hope that this book may be a stepping stone for those who find prayer difficult, for those who have no set pattern of prayer and for those who would like a fresh way of looking at their prayer life.

Prayer itself, however, is not a matter of just using a particular method or practical aid. Prayer is what happens when these methods are put into use for the purpose of building up our relationship with the Father, and I hope that somewhere in these pages, amongst the suggestions and the practicalities, there may be something that can help someone else to make further moves in the field of prayer. Our shattered world needs prayer, our tired and sick bodies need the touch of God, and peace needs to be restored to the fretful and anxious minds of so many people. To all of us Jesus Christ offers communion with God as a means of putting right our relationship with the Father and the world.

All Bible quotations are taken from the New International Version, and details of publications from which I have quoted may be found in the notes at the end of each chapter.

I would like to express my gratitude to Canon William Purcell of Mowbray's for making it possible for me to write this book, and also to the Reverend Richard Harries for his encouragement and willingness to write the foreword. I would also like to thank Mrs Julie Schofield for reading the manuscript and making many valuable suggestions and finally, above all, my wife Gillian, for all her hard work in typing the manuscript and keeping me going!

J.R.

1. What is prayer?

You're omniscient, God, and I'm stupid;
You're omnipotent and I'm weak;
You're eternal and I'm but a creature of a day.
Why don't You pick on someone Your own size?[1]

Every time I read through the Bible, God, I get the impression that You mellowed an awful lot as You got older.[2]

Who is God? What sort of God is it that Christians worship? If anyone were to read the Bible to find out the answer to these questions, it is more than likely the conclusions drawn would contain some of the following facts:

First, that God cares about his people, a fact demonstrated by sending his Son to earth for our sake. One of the most well loved Bible verses puts it like this:

For God so loved the world that he gave his one and only Son, that whoever believes in him shall not perish but have eternal life. (John 3.16)

Secondly, God is well able to look after us and is willing to help us in every situation in life. The Lord said to Jeremiah:

'I am the Lord, the God of all mankind. Is anything too hard for me?' (Jer. 32.27)

God's concern for us is something that Jesus also spoke about:

Consider the ravens: They do not sow or reap, they have no storeroom or barn; yet God feeds them. And

1

how much more valuable you are than birds! (Luke 12.24)

Thirdly, the Bible assures us that God is committed to us. Throughout the Bible there is evidence of this in the many covenants made between God and man. For example:

I will remember my covenant between me and you and all living creatures of every kind. Never again will the waters become a flood to destroy all life. (Gen. 9.15)

This is the covenant that I will make with the house of Israel . . . I will put my law in their minds and write it on their hearts. I will be their God, and they will be my people. (Jer. 31.33)

This is my blood of the covenant, which is poured out for many for the forgiveness of sins. (Matt. 26.28)

In addition the Gospels and the Epistles contain many references to the 'second coming'. Much has been written on the meaning of these words, but whatever the interpretation, the implication is that God is firmly committed to his people and that commitment involves Christ's return to them despite their failings and their rejection of him. This relationship between God and man could be summed up in Thomas Hardy's picture of marriage:

Whenever you look up, there I shall be — and whenever I look up, there will be you.[3]

However, love seeks a response and in this respect the love of God is no different from any other love — so God who is eager to show love to the world must also want this commitment to be returned, not from duty, but simply in gratitude. Prayer is that response to his love and commitment and can be summed up in three different areas: faith, action and fellowship.

Faith

Having faith in God is to believe in him, to know that he is always present, always loving, always caring and longing to help. So in the light of this we pray to God, taking to him the worries of this life, confidently knowing that he is listening. Responding in this way to God, however, means that it should not be just needs and desires that we take to him but also praise and thanksgiving for the work that he has already done. So this is one answer to the question, 'What is prayer?' Prayer involves believing in God to the extent that we can take to him all the things of this life, and ask him to work his power through them, and praising him for what he has already done.

Action

Responding to God in faith also involves action. If someone recognizes the reality of God in their life and the love and care that he has for them, it must surely follow that the same love and care applies to the rest of the world as well. But however much one accepts this, sometimes an individual can look at the distressing situations around him and be struck by a sense of helplessness. This is where prayer comes in. In prayer God can be approached about the world but, as we shall see in a later chapter, this is not the end of the matter. For if God answers prayer, then whoever is praying must be ready to be obedient to the call of God, and if needs be, to be an instrument through which that prayer is answered. First, however, there must be prayer. The first duty, the first action a Christian can undertake for the world, is to pray for it. The door leading into the chapel at Lincoln Theological College has an inscription on both sides. On one side it says 'To pray is to work', and on the other side it reads 'To work is to pray'. In other words, when the time of prayer is over, when Christians go out in the obedience of Christ to do his work, then God is still being honoured and his name is still being glorified as much as when prayers of adoration and hymns of praise ascend to his throne. It is often said that the image of the cross has two lines to it, one is vertical and goes from man to God and the other is horizontal and runs from man to man. Our relationship with God should be reflected in our relationship with other people, so that there will come a time when praying Christians should get up off their knees and act on their belief by showing practical help to those who need it. It is not enough to pray for those in need and then think that duty has been done. A Christian response means that prayer must be backed up by action. To love God in prayer means that we have to love our fellow human beings in action, as the first epistle of John says.

> If anyone says, 'I love God', yet hates his brother, he is a liar. For anyone who does not love his brother, whom he has seen, cannot love God, whom he has not seen. And he has given us this command: Whoever loves God must also love his brother. (1 John 4.20–21)

Fellowship

Finally, we respond to God by seeking fellowship with him. Being open to God creates a channel for him to act in our lives and in the world around us, but it is also a state of fellowship that can be enjoyed. God wants us to pray because prayer opens a door and draws us closer to him. Prayer not only does something — it *is* something. In the book of Revelation, chapter 3, verse 20, we read these words:

> Here I am! I stand at the door and knock. If anyone hears my voice and opens the door, I will go in and eat with him, and he with me.

What this verse is saying is that there is more to God than believing in his existence. There is more to God than wearing ourselves to the bone fighting for every good cause that

4

crosses our path. Prayer also means enjoying God to the fullest, sharing with him in love. This is also prayer: to rest with God and to experience his love for us by expressing our love for him.

Throughout this chapter we have looked at the question 'What is prayer?' Prayer is our attempt to communicate with God. It is not correct to hold up a book of prayers and say 'This is prayer', for they only become prayers in the true sense of the word when they are prayed. It is possible to read right through them without actually praying at all.

Prayer is faith, action and fellowship. It is more than muttering a few holy words. Prayer is the response of an individual to the existence of God and what he has done for the world.

God wants us to be honest in prayer. Honesty can be judged on two different levels: first of all, being true to ourselves. In his book *Prayers for Pagans and Hypocrites*, Peter de Rosa comments on the insincere side of church services:

> For I swear, I heard them in solemn Sunday rows pleading with God for what they desperately didn't want, confessing a hearty sorrow for sin they did not in the least feel and praising the Almighty when they passionately wanted to wring his sacred neck. Funniest of all, I suppose, were the bland appeals — loudest and clearest from the bourgeoisie — to be rendered poor and crucified.[4]

There is also the sense in which the praying person must be honest in what he is doing. In Luke 18 we read this parable:

> Two men went up to the temple to pray, one a Pharisee and the other a tax collector. The Pharisee stood up and prayed about himself: 'God, I thank you that I am not like all other men — robbers, evildoers, adulterers — or even like this tax collector. I fast twice a week and give a tenth of all I get.'
> But the tax collector stood at a distance. He would

5

not even look up to heaven, but beat his breast and said, 'God, have mercy on me, a sinner.'

I tell you that this man, rather than the other, went home justified before God. (Luke 18.10–14)

One of the things that this parable illustrates is what counts as prayer and what does not. The Pharisee extolled his own righteousness, and used his 'prayer time' to exalt himself, whereas the tax collector responded to the presence and the greatness of God, which took him to a position of genuine humility and repentance. There are hopefully few people who would dare to mirror the self-righteousness of the Pharisee in their prayers, but those who pray should recognize that whilst praying the attitude of their heart can either carry their prayers to the throne of God, or else render them all but useless. This is not to say that only 'good' people can pray, or that God only answers the prayers of the morally perfect, but anyone who prays must recognize that God sees our hearts and our attitudes, and these are as important to him as the words on our lips.

One of the great paradoxes of the Christian life is that on the one hand prayer is the greatest thing that we can do, but on the other it is also one of the most difficult tasks that we can set ourselves. It is rarely something that comes naturally. There are very few who achieve a state of constant dialogue with God in this life, the reason being that there are barriers between God and man, the infinite and the finite, the verbal and the non-verbal. Praying is not as easy as talking to a friend, and for this reason many people do not bother to pray at all. Prayer takes time, it involves wrestling with distractions in order to allow the spiritual world to enter the temporal. This does not mean that praying is always a marvellous experience. For most people praying is a matter of dutifully making the effort to shut out the world for a few moments and to concentrate on the business of God. However, if this is done with sincerity of heart and in recognition of our failings, we will surely be like the tax collector in that parable from Luke, and in the words of our Lord we will go home 'justified before God'.

Notes

1. Peter De Rosa, *Prayers for Pagans and Hypocrites*, William Collins Sons & Co. Ltd, London, 1977, p. 113

2. Ibid., p. 88

3. Thomas Hardy, *Far From the Madding Crowd*, Macmillan, 1974, p. 66

4. Peter De Rosa. *Prayers for Pagans and Hypocrites*, p. 6.

2. Settling down

Anybody who has ever sat down to paint a picture will realize that the most difficult part is actually putting the first pencil line, or the first splash of colour, on the canvas. Likewise if anyone has ever sat down to write an essay or a poem it is often those first few words that are the most difficult to write.

For many, the most difficult part of praying is actually using those first few words. For the artist or writer, careful planning and preparation can help to remove their fear, as they begin to visualize the finished picture on the canvas or the format of the essay. So it is with those of us who wish to pray. A few moments of preparation can help with that difficult task of talking to God and pouring out our hearts to him. So let us look at some of the initial hurdles that can be cleared to help create a state of mind where prayer begins to happen.

When and where to pray

One of the most common questions about prayer is 'When should I pray?' This can mean one of two things; either 'When is the best time to pray?' or 'How can I find time to pray?' The two questions are, however, of a similar nature.

For some, the best time to pray is the early morning, fresh from sleep, fresh from pressures and able to pray for the day ahead. Others might prefer the evening or last thing at night, when time can be spent looking back over what has happened during the day. It depends on the individual, for there is no part of the day that is holier, or better suited to prayer, than any other. The best time to pray is when it is easiest and most convenient to do so.

However, some people lead such busy lives that they would be grateful for two minutes to call their own. Here then are a few examples of how a time for prayer may be fitted into a busy daily routine.

Those who work full-time may feel that due to their long working hours and family commitments, they have no time at all to be on their own. Yet if they work in a city or town, a few minutes of their lunch hour spent in a nearby church can provide a chance to be alone, undisturbed, and in a prayerful atmosphere. Others may have a few solitary minutes in the house before leaving for work, and by careful, and sometimes cunning, reorganization this time may be used for prayer. Commuters may find that they are able to pray while travelling. Even if the bus is not a solitary place to pray, they can usually be undisturbed and guaranteed a fairly fixed period of time with their own thoughts. Edward England tells of how he always used to listen to the car radio on his drive into work, but then began to use this time for prayer instead:

> So instead of turning on my radio I used this journey as a period for worshipping God and saying my prayers. It was the start of a new pattern. Within a few days I had completely stopped turning on the car radio in the morning. The car became my sanctuary.
>
> With the windows tightly closed, my voice so unmelodious, I sang 'Fear not, rejoice, and be glad!' Sometimes the glory of God filled the car.[1]

There are, however, those who are going to find it nearly impossible to find even a few minutes in which to pray: for example, mothers with small children. It is said that Susannah Wesley would pull her apron over her face when she wanted to pray, and her children were instructed not to disturb their mother at such a time. Lucky the mother who can get away with that today! For those for whom it is difficult to find even the shortest of times to devote to prayer, the section on 'Arrow Prayers' in Chapter Six might be of some use.

Perhaps a word should be said about the danger of praying only 'when we feel like it'. Naturally we will feel more like praying at some times than at others, but if we rely solely on our feelings to inspire us, then there will be large periods of our life with no prayer at all. Jean Darnell wrote this about moods and prayer:

> My moods affect my way of praying. At times I'm articulate and feel my faith, my joy and can express it fluently. Other times, I'm hardly able to speak and feel nothing. Yet, whatever the mood, I know I'm accepted and loved.[2]

On the same subject, Harry Williams spoke of his time in a monastic community, and it is not difficult to relate the experiences of his way of life to our times and moods of prayer.

> There were occasionally days when it felt rewarding, leaving a warm glow in the heart. There were other days when the temperature dropped considerably. . . . But I went on none the less, because somewhere within me I knew that in spite of appearances I was on the road to fulfilment and joy.[3]

To a large extent, the question of where to pray is determined by when we pray. Not everyone enjoys the luxury of being able to go into a separate room to ensure silence and privacy. Many people pray on the bus or on the train, and more un-cell-like places than these it is hard to imagine. Some may find the atmosphere of a church very conducive to prayer and at the same time feel a part of the whole body of praying Christians. Others, however, prefer to pray where the glory of God is immediately visible in his creation — contemplating a beautiful view can give them a real sense of being part of that creation. For this purpose, several modern churches and chapels have been constructed so that the worshippers inside can see the world outside. However, no particular piece of countryside, building or cathedral is *the* right place to pray: wherever we feel able to pray is a good place, whether it be in a church, in a field or even in the bath! The actual physical location is unimportant, it may well depend on what is available at the time. God is not confined to any one place — he is everywhere — so there is nowhere prayer cannot be heard and no time when it is inappropriate to pray.

Posture and length of prayer

Derick Bingham writes this about his ways of praying:

> I go, sometimes, for 'praying walks', praying inwardly all the time I am out walking, pouring out my soul to the Lord. Sometimes I pray on the flat of my stomach on the study floor. Sometimes I kneel in prayer, sometimes I stand. Sometimes I shut my eyes in prayer, sometimes I don't.[4]

The question of whether it is best to stand or kneel in prayer is quite unimportant. The Bible mentions various postures associated with prayer, such as bowing the head, kneeling, standing, or even lying prostrate. None of these is any better or any worse than any other: it is purely a matter of taste, comfort and convenience. The traditions of different churches will probably play a part here, as will the general considerations of age and flexibility! It is helpful however to choose a suitable and comfortable position and then stick to it, so that it becomes associated in our minds with prayers. Whenever that position is adopted, we are immediately reminded of what we are trying to do; this can have the effect of focusing our attention right from the very beginning, and hopefully we will be less inclined to daydream! Jerome Lantry, a Roman Catholic priest, speaks of the need of keeping to a set pattern:

> . . . changing place, time or posture may give a brief 'lift' to our prayer for a while but the patient perseverance with the one way of praying does more to deepen the awareness.[5]

11

Another common question about prayer is 'How long should our prayers last?' This is rather like asking 'How long is a piece of string?' There is no hard and fast rule. Ideally we can never pray for too long, but that does not help a busy person who wishes to start a life of prayer. It is simply a question of breaking ourselves in gradually. There is little point at the beginning in deciding to sit down and pray for three hours, for it is unlikely that even a third of that time could be achieved without finding it monotonous, and far from the joyful experience we would like it to be. Of course there are those who can pray for three hours and more without ceasing, but it is unlikely that they have done so from the beginning. At the other end of the scale, five minutes is probably not long enough, as it does not give sufficient time for all the different elements of prayer to be included. As a guideline, perhaps between ten and fifteen minutes would be a good length of time to set aside, and perhaps, in time, we may find ourselves spending even longer in prayer.

Beginning our prayers

Some of the basic worries about prayer have now been discussed and we are ready to begin to pray, but it is not always that simple. Anyone who has ever played a sport will know how important it is to warm up the body first. It is not simply a matter of being keen and willing; the body must be prepared for what is going to happen or else very soon strain and stress will set in. This is why athletes go through a period of limbering up before beginning their sport. People who wish to pray could learn a lot from this. All too often we launch straight into our prayers without any mental switch from what we were doing before, and consequently our minds are full of random thoughts and distractions which soon begin to encroach upon our prayers. Therefore prayer time should always begin with a period of preparation. This may not in itself make us feel any more prayerful; as Richard Harries says:

All that is necessary . . . is a mental reminder that God is present. . . . If this mental act brings a feeling in its wake, well and good. If it doesn't, it doesn't matter in the slightest.[6]

All that is happening in this important period of time is that the mind is being allowed to readjust from what it was doing before and to enter into an attitude of prayer. George Stewart says:

'Enter into thy closet and shut the door', says Christ. There may be a good many doors to shut, other than that which keeps spectators away: and I suggest first that the usual attitude of prayer be taken and the mind withdrawn from its hold on anything.[7]

Here are some ways in which this transition may be achieved.

First of all, one could simply use a few moments in silence. William Law writes this:

The first thing that you are to do when you are upon your knees is to shut your eyes and with a short silence let your soul place itself in the presence of God; that is, you are to use this or some other better method to separate yourself from all the common thoughts and make your heart as sensible as you can of the divine presence.[8]

This silence can be coupled with a pattern of gentle breathing. Just a minute or two spent in this way at the beginning of a time of prayer can gently relax the body and help the mind to clear itself of the tensions which so easily build up within us all.

A second method of effecting the transition between a busy life and a time of prayer is to sing a hymn quietly. At any church service, one of the first things the congregation does is to sing a hymn, and this can help them to forget the rush of preparing for church and all the worries of that morning, and to achieve a better state of mind in which to concentrate on the worship of God. Private prayers could benefit greatly from following a similar pattern. All that is required is to find a hymn, or chorus, of praise and adoration, and simply sing it quietly. On occasions it may seem as if we are reading the words for the first time. Part of this is no doubt due to the fact that it does not matter about speed or pitch, for we can sing it just as we like. In this way an old hymn may come alive and enrich our prayers. Hopefully, during this time we will achieve a more peaceful frame of mind with which to continue in our prayers, for in that simple act of adoration prayer has already begun.

A third method of preparing for prayer is by using the Psalms. Psalms differ from hymns and from other parts of the Bible in that they can be seen as prayers in themselves. It is interesting to note that near the beginning of most set forms of morning and evening prayer there usually occurs an opportunity to say a selection of Psalms in addition to the normal time set aside for Bible reading. The Psalms are a collection of songs, poems and prayers from the ancient Jewish religion, which between them encompass the entire range of human emotions. There are Psalms of deep joy:

The Lord is my shepherd, I shall lack nothing. He makes me lie down in green pastures, he leads me beside quiet waters, he restores my soul (Psalm 23);

Psalms of praise:

Praise the Lord. How good it is to sing praises to our God, how pleasant and fitting to praise him! (Psalm 147);

Psalms of sorrow and repentance:

Have mercy on me, O God, according to your unfailing love; according to your great compassion blot out my transgressions. Wash away all my iniquity and cleanse me from my sin (Psalm 51);

and there are Psalms of desperation:

O Lord, hear my prayer, listen to my cry for mercy; in your faithfulness and righteousness come to my relief (Psalm 143);

My God, my God, why have you forsaken me? Why are you so far from saving me, so far from the words of my groaning? (Psalm 22)

The Psalms are marvellous pieces of literature to read as so often they seem to sum up the feelings and emotions that we so desperately try to express for ourselves. Reading them slowly enables their words to be punctuated with our own prayers and expressions of joy or sorrow, and so help to lift the weight of our cares from us. Often we may approach our prayer time in the wrong frame of mind. There may be tiredness and tension, or even anger or upset. In situations such as these, saying a Psalm can be a marvellous tonic because whereas resentment can linger and dominate us completely, by saying a Psalm we can throw all our emotions into it, and so, we hope, have the burden lifted from us.

William Law sums this up very clearly:

. . . there is nothing that so clears a way for your prayers, nothing that so disperses dullness of heart, nothing that so purifies the soul from poor and little passions, nothing that so opens heaven or carries your heart so near it as these songs of praise.

They create a sense and delight in God, they awaken holy desires, they teach you how to ask, and they prevail with God to give. They kindle a holy flame, they turn your heart into an altar, your prayers into incense, and carry them as a sweet-smelling savour to the throne of grace.[9]

Once we have spent some time in preparation and can feel calm before God, we are ready to move on to our prayer time itself.

Notes

1. Edward England, *My Path of Prayer*, (ed. David Hanes), Henry E. Walter, 1981, p. 34
2. Jean Darnell, ibid. p. 26
3. H. A. Williams, *Some Day I'll Find You*, Fount, 1984 (first published by Mitchell Beazley International), p. 362
4. Derick Bingham, *My Path of Prayer*, p. 19
5. Jerome Lantry OCD, *Saint Teresa on Prayer*, ed. by Thomas Curran OCD, Carmelite Centre of Spirituality, Living Flame Series 1981, p. 24
6. Richard Harries, *Turning to Prayer*, Mowbray, 1981, p. 98
7. George S. Stewart, *The Lower Levels of Prayer*, SCM Press, 1939, p. 28
8. William Law, *A Serious Call to a Devout and Holy Life*, SPCK, 1978, p. 198
9. Ibid., p. 210

3. What do we pray for?

There is a poster showing a crowd of penguins all milling about, going in different directions and the caption reads: 'Now that we're organized what shall we do?' Once the basic issue of where and when to pray have been considered, and a certain time for preparation has been taken into account, we could well say that this caption applies to us. What is the next step?

The next step is simply to begin to pray, but before launching straight into our prayers, it is wise to spend just a few minutes planning ahead. If prayers are garbled and without much continuity or structure they can become tiresome; it can seem as if they are being thrown against a brick wall. God no doubt listens to all prayers, no matter what order they come in, but it is beneficial to have a certain amount of structure to one's prayer life — so that prayers may be approached in an orderly and settled manner, with the correct priorities in prayer emphasized. It does not say much about our level of devotion if the first thing brought before God is a long list of personal wishes and desires. A simple pattern can ensure that prayer flows easily and reverently.

In church most services follow a similar order: a hymn of praise followed by a time of confession, then after hearing a reading from the Bible, a period of intercession, thanksgiving and so on. It is not particularly important that different denominations may slightly alter the order; what is significant is the standard content of most forms of worship — praise, confession, thanksgiving and intercession.

Praise

Before God is asked for anything, or thanked for anything, it is only proper that some time is spent remembering exactly who it is we are addressing. This is praise. To listen to some people praising God one would imagine that they were trying to flatter him, before bombarding him with requests, so that he will look more favourably on what they want. Praise is not flattering God but rather offering to him what is rightfully his. Augustine spoke about this in a prayer to God about man:

> The thought of you stirs him so deeply that he cannot be content unless he praises you, because you made us for yourself and our hearts find no peace until they rest in you.[1]

Such sentiments are very noble, but praising God can be a very difficult thing to put into practice without it feeling forced or laboured in some way. There are two aspects of praise, neither of which is better than the other, but which complement each other well. One is verbal praise, and the other is adoration.

Verbal praise involves recognizing God's attributes and articulating them. The words of the Te Deum illustrate this beautifully:

> We praise thee, O God: we acknowledge thee to be the Lord.
> All the earth doth worship thee: the Father everlasting.
> To thee all angels cry aloud: the Heavens and all the Powers therein.
> To thee Cherubin and Seraphin: continually do cry,
> Holy, Holy, Holy: Lord God of Sabaoth;
> Heaven and earth are full of the majesty: of thy Glory.

A great hymn of praise such as this makes us increasingly aware of the power and majesty of God. This is the point of verbal praise: that man, being small and finite can reach up and be aware of the greatness of God around him.

18

To begin with, we may feel so insignificant before God, that we do not know how to begin to praise him. A helpful idea might be to praise different attributes of God on different days; for example, on one day we might contemplate his majesty or kingship, on another day his love, and on another his power, and so on.

The other aspect of praise is adoration, where the emphasis is on resting in the glory of God. Through verbal praise the worshipper has been allowed to enter the presence of God, and now in adoration can rest in that same presence. There are practical ways in which this adoration, this resting in God, can be aided. William Law suggests this:

> Be still and imagine to yourself that you saw the heavens open and the glorious choirs of cherubims and seraphims about the throne of God. Imagine that you hear the music of those angelic voices that cease not to sing the glories of Him that is, and was, and is to come . . . imagine yourself amongst those heavenly companions, that your voice is added to theirs, and that angels join with you and you with them.[2]

This aspect of praise is not something that we consciously do; rather it is something that we are caught up in. For many people music is a very real means of transporting them into the presence of God, and there is no reason why, if this is the case, it should not be used in private devotions as well. However, this is not for everybody, and great care should be taken lest the time of praise be turned into an opportunity for listening to our favourite records!

Confession

Almost every church service includes a corporate form of confession. However because no two people are alike and all have different backgrounds and different daily routines, the wording of such a confession has to be very general indeed, so that everybody can in some way identify with it. As a result, it is quite common to reach the end of the confession without feeling that anything at all has been confessed. Our own private prayer of confession should be prevented from falling into the same trap. A good way of doing this is to make that time of confession as personal and as specific as possible. This can be done by going over the past day in chronological order, trying to bring back to mind all the things that have been said or done that may have caused others to suffer in any way, or things that have grieved God. The more specific the confession the more specific will be the forgiveness. Doing this daily can help us to live in a manner more suited to servants of God.

Even with the best intention in the world, however, simply going through this daily routine of remembering the past day's failings will eventually lose its crispness and some failings will slip through the net. Hence it is very useful once a fortnight, or at some regular convenient time, to set aside a separate period during which we can allow ourselves to be examined further by a different spiritual exercise. In his book *True Prayer*,[3] Kenneth Leech gives an example of such an exercise. He explains how to use the Beatitudes of Matthew 5.1–11 as a form of self-examination. The idea is to read each beatitude slowly in turn, and after each one, to meditate upon it to see if it brings to mind any personal sin. For example, the first beatitude is 'Blessed are the poor in Spirit'. As he dwells upon these words, the reader should try to imagine what Jesus meant by them and examine himself to see how he measures up to what Jesus was trying to say. Then the other Beatitudes should be considered in the same way.

There are other biblical passages which can be used to complement a daily pattern of confession. 1 Corinthians 13 contains the very beautiful hymn of love, and everyone could benefit greatly from setting aside some time to read slowly through it, in order that it might expose our failure to treat our fellow men with the practical considerations that love demands. Another humbling passage can be found in Galatians 5, where Paul contrasts the fruits of the Spirit — love, joy, peace etc. — (verses 22–23) with the works of the flesh (verses 19–21). We may read through these passages and despair of ever doing anything right because of all the sins and weaknesses they bring to mind, but it is only when we begin to recognize our sinfulness, that we can begin to experience forgiveness.

Yet another means of enhancing our daily routine of confession, in addition to reviewing the past day, is to look at the 'seven deadly sins' — pride, covetousness, lust, envy, greed, anger and sloth — and study one each day of the week. This will reveal the hold that these sins may have on us, and show us more clearly where forgiveness is needed. Thomas á Kempis says:

> If each year we would root out one fault, we should soon become perfect.[4]

Finally, there is one more aspect of confession that should never be overlooked, and that is the issue of forgiveness, our forgiveness of other people. In Mark 11.25, we read these words.

> And whenever you stand praying, if you hold anything against anyone, forgive him, so that your Father in heaven may forgive you your sins.

In a daily time of confession, as well as a review of what we have done wrong, there should also be a consideration of the ways others have wronged us. For each incident there should be a definite thought of forgiveness. As well as fulfilling a specific command of our Lord's, such an act greatly increases our awareness of the pain involved in forgiveness, and this will hopefully serve as a deterrent to sin.

Thanksgiving

The practice of thanking God for the blessings of this life is all too often omitted from personal prayer, not because of

21

a lack of gratitude for what has been received, but simply because it does not occur to many people to include it in their private prayers. There are two main reasons why there should be an element of thanksgiving in prayer time. The first is because it should be a natural part of life to say 'thank you'. Richard Harries says:

> Unlike us God is not standing on tiptoe to see if anyone is going to notice him; unlike us God is not greedy for recognition. So why should we offer thanks? There is only one answer: because we want to.[5]

In his book *The Hour that Changes the World*,[6] Dick Eastman calls thanksgiving 'a confession of blessings'. So just as a confession can be made by recalling the events of the past day, so a time of thanksgiving can be based on the same pattern, as we remember before God all the good things that have happened, the friends that we have made, our moments of joy, and the lessons we have learned. Done regularly this will soon create in us an increased awareness of the presence of God amidst the daily routine of life.

Merlin Carothers has outlined in his book *Prison to Praise*[7] his own personal practice of taking quite literally the biblical verses Romans 8.28:

> And we know that in all things God works for the good of those who love him

and 1 Thessalonians 5.18:

> . . . give thanks in all circumstances.

He tells of how, instead of grumbling about the things in his life that seemed to go wrong, he started to thank God for them. As a result he began to see new opportunities for pastoral care and evangelism. Whilst some people may have difficulties with the logical conclusions of this — for example, in what sense can we truly thank God for the armies of Hitler, or the rule of Idi Amin? — it is certainly true that we do not give thanks nearly as much as we should, and some time each day spent in this way would be of great value.

The second reason for offering thanks to God is in order to consecrate our lives to him, as Neville Ward explains:

It is Christian conviction that life . . . can be made meaningful and holy. Thankfulness consecrates it, makes it meaningful and holy. Jesus and his friends were brought up in a world of thought in which to bless a thing and give thanks for it were one and the same. The idea is familiar in Christian tradition in grace before meals. The meal is blessed, that is to say, made holy, when God is thanked for it. Life is also blessed and made holy when it is received with thankfulness.[8]

By thanking God for the things in this life, he is acknowledged as their source, and is thus placed at the centre of our lives.

Intercession

Some Christians claim that when they pray they never use prayers of intercession, either for other people or for themselves (normally called petition). The suggestion is that they are somehow 'above' such forms of prayer. However, prayer without asking is not biblical, for Jesus says:

Ask and it will be given to you; seek and you will find; knock and the door will be opened to you. (Matt. 7.7)

Again he says in John 15.7:

If you remain in me and my words remain in you, ask whatever you wish, and it will be given you.

A little later we will be looking at ways of helping our faith and perseverance in intercession, but for the moment let us spend some time looking at the whole question of making requests of God. Many problems and questions about intercession stem from the fact that many of us generally regard God as a powerful super-human who needs to be persuaded to do things which otherwise he would not do. Often we pray as though we were trying to justify our actions to God and persuade him to bless them. The great evangelist D. L. Moody described such occasions:

> We hear a good deal of praying that is just exhorting God, and if you did not see the man's eyes closed, you would suppose that he was preaching. Much that is called prayer is not prayer at all.[9]

Intercession is not trying to enlist God's help in a cause, nor persuading him to act in a certain way — rather it is acknowledging God's reign over us and submitting ourselves to his will. What then of all the biblical exhortations that we should ask in prayer? Jesus says this in John 5.19:

> Truly, truly, I say to you, the Son can do nothing of his own accord, but only what he sees the Father doing; for whatever he does, that the Son does likewise.

In other words, because of the unique relationship between the Father and the Son, Jesus knew his Father's will for the world and therefore was able to set his own hands to that work, consequently bringing about great healings and miracles. This surely is the key to intercession: that as far as possible, the Christian should seek to know God's will and join him in the work that he is doing in the world. Neville Ward put it this way:

> The Christian in prayer does not wish to persuade God to do anything other than what he is in fact continually doing — fulfilling his purpose in love. He simply wants himself to participate more fully in what God is doing.[10]

It is an exciting prospect to be able to pray in conformity with God's will and then see marvellous things happening in our lives.

There are two very important questions that confront us head on. The first is 'How do we know what God's will is so that we can pray in conformity with it?' Alas, here there is no easy answer. Indeed if there were such an answer, then the power of prayer would in no way be lacking. The Charismatic movement and the Quaker movement have both taught the modern Church a great deal about relying on the Holy Spirit for leadership in prayer. Often at charismatic meetings there is a time of silence before any prayer is spoken aloud, to give the Holy Spirit an opportunity to inspire and guide the intercessions. This is a discipline that many of us could benefit from in our individual prayer lives, as too often our own words are spoken without any thought for what the Spirit might be trying to say. Therefore, before beginning our intercessions, we should be silent. This involves blocking out all the sounds and distractions around us, and totally emptying our minds, so that we may wait more expectantly for the guidance for our prayers. Certain techniques can be used to help us in this, and these will be mentioned later, in Chapter Six.

All this, however, confronts us with the second question, 'How should we pray when we receive no specific guidance from God, but when situations confront us that demand our attention in prayer?'

The key to such prayer lies in the words of Jesus in John 14.14:

You may ask me for anything *in my name*, and I will do it.

Colin Urquhart suggests a way in which these words 'in my name' should be interpreted:

As you face a situation that requires prayer, you can ask yourself these questions:
1. How would Jesus love in this situation?
   That is the way I want to love.
2. What would Jesus do in this situation?
   That is what I want to do.

3. What would Jesus believe in this situation?
   That is how I want to believe.[11]

He adds:

> To pray 'in the name of Jesus' means that you bring
> Him into the prayer. He prays along with you. He
> approaches the problem with you. You face it together,
> in His power, with His faith.[12]

One further point should be made about intercession.
Almost every book written on the practice of Christian
prayer rightly stresses that there must be a strong relationship between the prayers that are prayed and the life that
is lived. As Neville Ward puts it:

> The test of the value of one's prayer is the kind of life
> one lives when one is not formally praying.[13]

This has serious implications, for example, we may repeatedly pray for the racial problems of the world, or for
the poor of the world (and the Sunday morning intercessions have a familiar ring to them, as again and again the
problems of the world are lifted up to the throne of God),
but is this *all* that we can do? James 2.15–16 reads as
follows:

> Suppose a brother or sister is without clothes and daily
> food. If one of you says to him, 'Go, I wish you well;
> keep warm and well fed', but does nothing about his
> physical needs, what good is it?

What the author is saying is that it is no good just saying
Christian words unless the words are backed up by a
willingness to act. We would do well to remember this in
our prayers. For example, it is no good praying for racial
harmony whilst bearing a grudge or prejudice against
people of a different race. A repentance of such feelings is
necessary for sincere prayer. We can go even further and
offer ourselves to be used as an answer to our own prayers.

Where we might pray: 'Father heal the differences between black people and white people', it would be better to pray 'Father take me to a situation of racial trouble, be it in a home or at school, and let me take your reconciling love into that situation'. Where we might ask God, in a general way, that 'all men may come to a knowledge of Christ's saving power', surely it would be more effective to ask: 'Lord, give me the opportunity to witness to somebody today.' To pray in this way is to become more and more bound up with what we are praying for. Naturally not all situations adapt themselves to this approach (and it would be difficult to mould every prayer to this pattern), but often it is worth looking at the general concerns in our prayers and trying to re-fashion them in more constructive ways.

Being quiet

Finally, it is important to include in one's daily time of prayer a period set aside for quiet, in which no words are offered and no sound is made, but the body and soul rest in silent expectation before God. In Chapter Six, we will be examining ways of achieving this. However, it must be said that of all the different elements which go into making up a balanced prayer life, the practice of being still before God is the most neglected, partly due to the fact that it is the most difficult to put into practice in our busy routines.

At first, the idea of spending ten to fifteen minutes in prayer may have seemed a long time. The time has, however, been divided into six sections: preparation, praise, confession, thanksgiving, intercession and being quiet. In order to try to fit all this into that period of time, only a little over two minutes can be spent on each section, which is hardly a difficult task. Hopefully, as this pattern is moulded and developed to individual requirements, the length of time that is set aside for prayer will gradually increase and each person will find a length of time that is suitable to them. With a small amount of practice, dividing up our prayer time in the way described can make our prayers more enjoyable. We all know how exhausting it is to listen to someone talking when they have no real structure to what they are saying — so it is with prayer time. Prayers without structure can be very tiring and will therefore deter us from praying the next day. As our prayer life develops, there is no reason why it should not be divided up to allow different sections to be prayed at different times of the day. In *The Imitation of Christ*,[14] Thomas á Kempis suggests that we pray twice a day; in the morning the emphasis should be on dedication, and in the evening, on self-examination. According to William Law, prayer should be offered five times during the day, starting at five o'clock in the morning![15] On each occasion, he suggests a different aspect of prayer should be emphasized: praise, humility, intercession, thanksgiving and submission, and finally a period of confession to end the day. Our own practice of prayer will soon reveal the pattern that is easiest, most convenient and most enjoyable for us, and we will be joyful Christians indeed if we can look forward with longing to the time we spend in prayer.

Notes

1. Saint Augustine, *Confessions*, translated by R. S. Pine-Coffin, Penguin 1977, Book 1, Chapter 1, p. 21

2. William Law, *A Serious Call to a Devout and Holy Life*, SPCK, 1978, p. 222

3. Kenneth Leech, *True Prayer*, Sheldon Press, 1980, p. 136f

4. Thomas á Kempis, *The Imitation of Christ*, translated by Leo Sherley-Price, Penguin Classics, 1983, p. 38

5. Richard Harries, *Turning to Prayer*, Mowbray, 1984, p. 18

6. Dick Eastman, *The Hour that Changes the World*, Baker Book House, 1979

7. Merlin Carothers, *Prison to Praise*, Hodder & Stoughton Ltd, 1970

8. J. Neville Ward, *The Use of Praying*, Epworth 1968, p. 21

9. D.L. Moody, *Prevailing Prayer*, Chicago: Moody Press, p. 18 — quoted by D. Eastman, ibid., p. 91

10. J. Neville Ward, *The Use of Praying*, p. 51

11. Colin Urquhart, *Anything You Ask*, Hodder & Stoughton Ltd, 1978, p. 125

12. Ibid.

13. J. Neville Ward, *The Use of Praying*, p. 30

14. Thomas á Kempis, *The Imitation of Christ*, translated by Leo Sherley-Price, Penguin Classics, 1983

15. William Law, *A Serious Call to a Devout and Holy Life*, SPCK, 1978

4. Persevering in prayer

In the last chapter, we examined the different elements which make up a balanced prayer life. For most people, however, the form of prayer which will receive the most emphasis is that of intercession. As a result, further questions on this subject need to be looked at. First, how do we persevere in our prayers? Most of us are aware that not every prayer is answered by God after praying for it only once. Often much perseverance and patience is required. However such perseverance can easily become monotonous and become counter-productive. How can we prevent this happening? Secondly, no one can be unaware of the vast quantity of situations and people that need prayer. Even if a person were to confine their prayers to the immediate concerns around them, they would soon be swamped by the enormity of the task confronting them. But how is it possible to be sincere in *all* our petitions? Thirdly, many of the things that we would like to pray for are large topics. How is it possible then, to turn our general feelings into specific prayers? Finally, what can be done about the despair that grips us when many a well-intentioned prayer seems to go unanswered?

Keeping at our prayers

Jerome Lantry writes this:

> Prayer is a part of our life and has its bright days and dull periods for many reasons. No one has ever achieved anything in any field without a lot of patience and real slogging.[1]

It is true that many of man's greatest achievements are not ones that have come easily, whether they be in sport, works of art, or other skills, and often much patience and perseverance is needed to reach the end result. Prayer is no different: it requires time and hard work before a person can begin to see the benefit in their life.

St Luke's Gospel contains two parables about persevering in prayer. They are quite similar in nature and serve a similar purpose.

Then he said to them, 'Suppose one of you has a friend, and he goes to him at midnight and says, "Friend, lend me three loaves of bread, because a friend of mine on a journey has come to me, and I have nothing to set before him".

'Then the one inside answers, "Don't bother me. The door is already locked, and my children are with me in bed. I can't get up and give you anything". I tell you, though he will not get up and give him the bread because he is his friend, yet because of the man's persistence he will get up and give him as much as he needs.

'So I say to you: "Ask and it will be given to you."'

(Luke 11.5–9a)

Then Jesus told his disciples a parable to show them that they should always pray and not give up. He said: 'In a certain town there was a judge who neither feared God nor cared about men. And there was a widow in that town who kept coming to him with the plea, "Grant me justice against my adversary".'

'For some time he refused. But finally he said to himself, "Even though I don't fear God or care about men, yet because this widow keeps bothering me, I will see that she gets justice, so that she won't eventually wear me out with her coming!"'

And the Lord said, 'Listen to what the unjust judge says. And will not God bring about justice for his chosen ones, who cry out to him day and night?'

(Luke 18. 1–7a)

These parables have certain features in common: in both of them there is someone in need and someone in a position to fulfil that need. There is also at first an unwillingness to act, which in the end is overcome by persistence.

Jesus told these parables to encourage us to be persistent in prayer. This is not because God is unwilling to act on our behalf; far from it, for as William Barclay says:

> If a churlish and unwilling householder can in the end be coerced by a friend's shameless persistence into giving him what he needs, how much more will God who is a loving Father supply all his children's needs.[2]

One reason why we should persist in prayer may have more to do with us than with God. Sometimes we may be so concerned about a coming event, or a situation in which we find ourselves, that we cannot progress to any other prayers until this particular situation has been voiced and pleaded. In this way we are sharing with a friend the deepest concerns of our lives. By continually praying about them, we allow ourselves to pass beyond them to face other facets of life.

Another reason to persevere in prayer is because we are co-workers with God. God did not create us as robots, with no independence of our own. His plan for the world does not work itself out independently of us; if that were so, then there would be no need for prayer at all. God wants us to share his concern for those in need, and through our prayers to release his power in their lives. Thus his purposes can be fulfilled and we have had the privilege of being labourers with him, and all of God's creation can be seen working together to fulfil his purposes.

However, repeatedly praying for something can become very monotonous if we don't seem to see any result. In whatever we attempt in life, though, there is a risk that it will lose its freshness and initial thrill. This applies to many things, whether it be setting out on a long walk, painting a picture, or praying. In each case, though, the final goal is potentially thrilling, and it is important to keep it always in sight to encourage us to persevere. With prayer, the goal is the development of our relationship with God, and the releasing of his power in our lives and in the lives of those we are praying for.

The question still remains of how to persevere in prayer without merely resorting to dull and vainless repetition? In everyone's life, there are bound to be circumstances that warrant specific prayer. Let us take three examples; perhaps a friend is ill, a broken relationship needs healing, and there is anxiety about the future. These should all be written down on a piece of paper in as much detail as possible. This piece of paper could be used as a bookmark in a Bible or any other book which is read regularly. Then, daily, each one of these topics should be prayed for, not in a way that beseeches God to act in the way that *we* want, but rather in a way that surrenders to him all the aspects of the situation known to us, and our involvement in that particular situation. This is normally quite easy to achieve for a short period of time, about a week or a fortnight, but after that monotony can begin to creep in. To combat this, it can be a good idea to change the direction of the prayers after a while. This can be done by taking that same piece of paper and writing at the top of it, 'What God is doing in my life'. By doing this, our prayers can undergo quite a lift, since when we look at the piece of paper, it ceases to be a reminder of our three problems, but rather a reminder of the power of God already present in our lives.

Keeping lists

As was mentioned earlier, one of the difficulties about intercession is knowing how to cope with the vast quantity of material that could be included without becoming completely swamped by it all.

One way round this is to draw up a prayer list. This is done simply by writing down on a piece of paper the names of all those for whom prayer would be appropriate. This list may contain three names, or it may contain thirty — it really does not matter. However, if each of these thirty people were to be prayed for every day, then it is likely that after a short period of time the names would be mentioned without much thought being given to any of their individual circumstances or needs. Rather, the emphasis would be on getting to the end of the list as soon as possible! Far better, then, to pray for three people each day with meaning and sincerity and spread the list over ten days. In this way some time each day can be spent praying about the specific needs and situations of each individual included. As a clergyman, I am issued with a cycle of prayer that encourages me to remember a different church and its ministers each day of the year. By using this list we are supported by each other in thought and prayer. It is also my responsibility to pray for those in my charge, so I keep a second cycle of prayer of my own, so that each day I am able to pray for four or five members of my congregation, as well as members of my family and friends. Praying in this manner has the advantage that there is always something fresh to put into our daily prayers, so that they do not become the same standard prayers day after day. Perhaps we may feel that only praying for somebody every ten days or fortnight is rather removed from the idea of persevering in prayer. However, several times in his letters, St Paul speaks of 'making mention' of his fellow Christians by name, suggesting that it is simply enough to lift the names of those in need before God, trusting him to bless each one of them.

The written list can also serve to remind us of those in need of prayer. The following scene from *The Sound of Music* may ring a few bells:

God bless the captain, God bless Liesl and Friedrich, God bless Louise, Briggita, Marta and little Gretl —

34

and oh, I forgot the other boy, what's his name? Well, God bless 'what's his name'.[3]

A prayer list can avoid spending too much time on deciding what to include, or trying to remember who needs special prayer. Some people also find it useful to carry around a piece of paper, so that when they come across something that needs prayer, they can simply jot it down and add it to their daily list. If we feel that the list itself is becoming too familiar in its order, then it is simple enough to throw all the names into a bag and start all over again, dividing them into new groups, perhaps praying for slightly more or less names each day. However it is also important to remember that it is possible to become enslaved to lists, and should the occasion ever arise when something else seems more important on one particular day, then that should take priority.

Breaking down our prayers

Another difficulty with intercessions is that they can become very general, and thus can very soon cease to be prayers as such, and become more like fanciful ideals for the state of the world. For example: 'We pray that the world might live in peace'. This is indeed a noble sentiment, but such a prayer can become difficult to identify and persevere with when it is phrased in such general terms. One way of overcoming this particular problem is to turn general desires into specific requests. Thus, if we wish to pray for the peace of the world, we would do well to read a daily newspaper and find out which troubled areas of the world most need our prayers. Perhaps we could choose a different geographical area each week and pray for particular aspects of the situation there: one day we could pray for the leaders, on the next day the population, then the physical hardships, our understanding of the situation, the children of the area, and so on. In this way, perseverance in prayer is balanced by an interest in the subject that is being prayed for.

35

Another method of breaking down our prayers is to pray in stages. The idea being that instead of just praying towards the end result, our prayers focus on the different stages that lead up to that same result. Let us look at an example of how this might work in practice. Let us imagine that we were due to take an examination. What is the best way to pray for something like that? Naturally, the prayer that springs most readily to mind is, 'God, let me do well in this exam'. However, we could go deeper than that and ask for God's blessing in each successive stage leading up to it. First, we could pray for God to give us a clear head for revision, to help us concentrate on what we are doing. When the revision has been done, the next stage is the examination day itself. At the beginning of the day we could pray that our nerves will not get the better of us as we prepare for the actual time of examination. Then we might pray for a safe journey to our destination, and that God will be with us and with all those taking the exam alongside us. Just before looking at any last minute notes, we might pray that he will help us recall all the facts that have been committed to the memory over the past weeks and months. Finally, in the minute before actually writing or before walking into the interview room, our final prayer may be to the effect that our minds may remain clear and the body refreshed as everything possible is given to the testing time that lies ahead.

In Mark 11.23–24, we read these words:

I tell you the truth, if anyone says to this mountain, 'Go throw yourself into the sea,' and does not doubt in his heart but believes that what he says will happen, it will be done for him. Therefore I tell you, whatever you ask for in prayer, believe that you have received it, and it will be yours.

William Barclay comments on the passage in this way:

It is the universal fact that anything tried in the spirit of confident expectation has a more than double chance of success. The patient who goes to a doctor and has no confidence in the prescribed remedies has far less chance of recovery than the patient who is confident that the doctor can cure him. When we pray, it must never be a mere formality, it must never be ritual without hope.[4]

Breaking down our prayers into stages can make it easier to believe that our prayers *could* be answered, as our faith is more able to deal with smaller hurdles, than larger ones. Thus, the 'confident expectation' that our prayers need can be injected into our petitions at each stage of our requests. This method can be particularly helpful when praying for things that cause anxiety; whether it be an illness, whereby prayers for healing can be broken down into stages, or a visit that has to be made, which is the source of some worry: One of the dangers of breaking one's prayers down into stages is that a person might find him or herself telling God exactly how he should be answering certain prayers, and by exactly what methods he is allowed to bring that answer about. God is sovereign, and by praying to him we are not dictating demands to him, but rather opening up to him all of the elements which go into any given situation that he might use all of them to bring about his ultimate glory and our ultimate joy.

Unanswered prayer

'Father, I know You always answer my prayers, but couldn't You sometimes say Yes?'[5]

'I've reached the stage now God, where I'm afraid to pray for the sun to rise in the mornings in case it doesn't.'[6]

There are many people who feel a close affinity with such prayers. They may be convinced that God hears their prayers, and sure that he has the ability to answer them.

The only problem is that he seems to be saying 'no' to most of them.

There is a sense, of course, in which there is no such thing as unanswered prayer, since even if the answer is 'no' then it is still an answer. William Barclay writes this:

> If we do not receive what we pray for, it is not because God grudgingly refuses to give it but because he has some better thing for us. There is no such thing as unanswered prayer. The answer given may not be the answer we desired or expected; but even when it is a refusal it is the answer of the love and wisdom of God.[7]

It has been said that God answers prayer in three ways — 'Yes', 'No' and 'Wait', and even if all of these constitute an answer to prayer, most people would like to see more of the 'Yes' and not so much of the 'No' or 'Wait'. So why is it that so often we receive negative answers to our prayers?

In the epistle of James we read these words:

> You do not have, because you do not ask God. When you ask, you do not receive, because you ask with wrong motives, that you may spend what you get on your pleasures. (James 4.2–3)

Of course God desires our happiness as much as we do, but unfortunately we are not always in the best position to judge what it is that can ensure our happiness. A child may ask for something from his parents thinking it will bring joy and happiness. The parents, however, are in a better position to judge the request and the consequences of fulfilling it. For example, a boy may want a bicycle, but the parents may refuse it for the best motives, perhaps because he is not old enough to cope with the dangers of cycling. So with God: often if our prayers seem to go unanswered it is because it would not be immediately beneficial for them to be granted in the way we would like. As one lady was heard to remark, 'God doesn't always answer our prayers exactly as we wish, otherwise I would have

38

married the wrong man many times'. Our prayers must therefore be open enough to allow God room to answer them in his way and not ours.

Another reason why we think we have not received answers to our prayers is because we do not recognize them when they come. Many times in church we hear prayers for the sick, but hardly ever do we hear God thanked for their recovery. We ask God to strengthen and heal them, but thanks are given to the doctors when healing takes place. Of course thanks are due to the nurses and doctors, but also to God as well. If God was not expected to have anything to do with the healing, then why were they prayed for in the first place? For God to answer prayers in the affirmative does not mean that supernatural events have to take place in our lives. It may be that the answer to prayer will come in a dramatic form, but more often than not it will happen quite naturally and can only be seen as an act of God through the eyes of faith.

Finally, our prayers may not receive a positive answer because our perseverance is lacking. It is interesting that twice we read of Jesus repeating his prayers to achieve the final result. In Mark 5.1–20, we read how Jesus cast a demon from a man by commanding it to leave over and over again (verse 8). Presumably his perseverance had something to do with the final outcome. Again, in Mark 8.22–26 Jesus healed a blind man. After the first prayer, the man was partially healed, but Jesus had to pray again to complete the healing. Often our prayers have to be repeated over a period of time before we obtain an answer, and many times we make the mistake of giving up before we receive that answer. Colin Urquhart graphically describes answers to prayer as being either 'Arrows' or 'Tortoises'; sometimes the answer arrives as quickly as an arrow, yet at other times it comes as slowly as a tortoise. He continues:

It is so easy to give up before the 'tortoise' arrives. And when you stop believing, the tortoise stops moving towards you. Its head shoots back into its shell! There the answer to your prayer remains, suspended somewhere between heaven and you.[8]

Whatever the reason behind what seems to be unanswered prayer, or behind prayers that always seem to receive the answer 'No', it is important to remember that all prayer is heard by God. As G.B. Caird writes:

> Jesus does not promise his disciples that they will always get what they ask, but he does assure them that they cannot ask, seek or knock in vain.[9]

One of the biggest mistakes a person can make is to stop praying because their prayers seem to go unanswered. It is like a racing driver who gives up racing because he is not winning all of the races, when what he should be doing is continuing with his driving until he starts to come in first. So it is with us. If for a while prayer may seem to make no difference, then we should carry on nevertheless. Sometimes we should try out new methods, sometimes persevering with more familiar ones, all the time questioning and seeking, trying to improve our relationship with God and maintaining our fervent desire to be channels of his love and will in this world.

Notes

1. Jerome Lantry OCD, *Saint Teresa on Prayer*, ed. by Thomas Curran OCD, Carmelite Centre of Spirituality, Living Flame Series, 1981, p. 23

2. William Barclay, *The Gospel of Luke*, The Daily Study Bible, The Saint Andrew Press, 1983, p. 146

3. *The Sound of Music.*

4. William Barclay, *The Gospel of Mark*, The Daily Study Bible, The Saint Andrew Press, 1984, p. 277

5. Peter de Rosa, *Prayers for Pagans and Hypocrites*, William Collins Sons & Co. Ltd., London, 1977, p. 43

6. Ibid., p. 44

7. William Barclay, *The Gospel of Luke*, p. 146

8. Colin Urquhart, *Anything You Ask*, Hodder & Stoughton Ltd, 1981, p. 115

9. G.B. Caird, *Saint Luke*, Penguin Books, 1977, p. 153

5. Helping our prayers

Even the greatest of saints have been afflicted by times when prayer seemed impossible. There are bound to be times in the life of everyone who prays when the words will not come, or when neither the energy nor the imagination are present to enable even the most devout person to focus his or her attention on God. St Teresa once wrote:

> Very often I was more occupied with the wish to see the end of my hour of prayer. I used to actually watch the sandglass, and the sadness that I sometimes felt on entering my prayer chapel was so great that it required all my courage to force myself inside. In the end, our Lord came to my help. And when I had persisted in this way I found far greater peace and joy than when I prayed with excitement and emotional rapture.[1]

At moments like this, an aid to prayer can be a great help. A wise spiritual director once told his pupils that there are bound to be times in any person's life when prayer is difficult, and at such times something is needed to carry our prayers to God, just as a train is carried by railway tracks. In this chapter we shall be looking at some practical ways of enriching our prayer time.

Set forms of prayer

Sunday services are, for the most part, worship presented in a fixed form. In the Church of England and the Roman Catholic Church this is presented in a printed book, whether it be for a service of Holy Communion or for

Morning or Evening Prayer. In the Free Churches there is also a recognizable pattern incorporating the familiar elements of praise, confession, intercession and the ministry of the word; so the pattern of worship is not picked at random but progresses on a steady journey from beginning to end. It can often be helpful to use these orders of service (called the Offices) in our daily prayer life, especially the forms of Morning and Evening Prayer, for several reasons. The first is that these forms of worship give a certain balance to our prayer time; following them makes sure that all the elements of praise, confession, intercession and so forth are included. They can also give expression to our praise and thanksgiving when we feel uninspired and are unable to find the correct words ourselves. William Law speaks of such moments when our hearts are dull and uninspired:

> It is therefore highly necessary to provide against this . . . by having at hand such forms of prayer as may best suit us when our hearts are in their best state, and also be most likely to raise and stir them up when they are sunk into dullness. For as words have a power of affecting our hearts on all occasions . . . so it is reasonable that we should make this advantage of language and provide ourselves with such forms of expression as are most likely to move and enliven our souls and fill them with sentiments suitable to them.[2]

So by using these forms of worship, we are helped to give expression to feelings which our emotions can easily dampen.

Secondly, using set forms of worship which others have carefully thought out, making them our own, can be a source of joy and inspiration in our prayer lives. How often we read in a poem or novel our own ideas and emotions outlined far more vividly and clearly than we could describe them, and the same can apply to our prayers. Saying a set form of confession with conviction can at times enable one to reflect more deeply about the nature of one's sins. Reading a set hymn of praise, such as the Te Deum (a part of which was quoted in Chapter Three), can reveal new aspects of the glory of God, and inspire our own attempts at praising God. Of course, it does not matter to God in the slightest whether prayers are couched in glorious phrases, or whether they are simply the first words that enter the mind; what is behind the words counts as much as the words themselves. But it can be a real help in times of dryness to know that our one solitary voice of prayer is being joined with the voice of others in a common language of praise, thanksgiving and inter-cession.

This leads to the third advantage of using the Offices in daily prayer life, which is the assurance it gives us that we are not alone at our prayers, but rather joining in a great fellowship of worshippers, many of whom will be using exactly the same form of prayers. Kenneth Leech talks about it in this way:

> It is a means by which we pray with the whole church, uniting our prayers with that of millions of other Chris-tians living and dead. This is true whether one is alone or with a group.[3]

Another advantage is that almost all of the offices require a portion of scripture to be read, and by the use of an accompanying lectionary or a table of readings, a wide selection of biblical passages is studied. Too often only the most appealing passages of scripture are read, or the ones best suited to our present state of emotions and in that way our knowledge of the Bible is never increased or enriched by the constant stimulation of something new and differ-ent. Using a lectionary can safeguard against this danger and ensure that the whole range of literature within the Bible is read.

It should be mentioned at this point that there are cer-tain things to watch out for when using these set forms of prayer over a lengthy period of time. When someone becomes accustomed to the words that are being read, it is all too easy to skim over them without a thought for their meaning. It is possible to reach the end of one section and then not remember what it was all about. A certain amount of concentration is necessary to make the discipline worthwhile. There is also the danger that these set forms of prayer will totally dominate the prayer life of an individual and that prayer will cease the moment the written prayers cease. There must always be an opportunity for personal expressions of praise, thanksgiving and intercession. One final thing that is worth bearing in mind is that there are a variety of different prayer books available and whilst it is unwise to fluctuate without giving each set form an opportunity to express itself within us, there is always the option to try a different form of service to increase the spiritual input in our prayer lives.

Using written prayers

Donald Coggan, a former Archbishop of Canterbury, wrote this in his foreword to *Parish Prayers*:

> We all know what it is to hit an arid patch in our prayer-life. At such a time it is of help to prime the pump of prayer with the aid of prayers of other, and greater, Christians.[4]

Apart from the Offices, there are other forms of written prayers available that can help with the structuring and content of a prayer time. George Appleton said:

> They help to push our little boat off from the bank into the main stream, when it gets carried on by the current almost without effort.[5]

In other words written prayers can form the basis of personal prayers; they can be added to, and personal references can be 'pegged' on to them. For example, one such prayer that might be used is that known as St Patrick's Breastplate, which goes as follows:

Christ be with me, Christ within me.
Christ behind me, Christ before me.
Christ beside me, Christ to win me.
Christ to comfort and restore me.
Christ beneath me, Christ above me.
Christ in quiet, Christ in danger.
Christ in hearts of all that love me,
Christ in mouth of friend and stranger.

By reading this prayer slowly and thoughtfully, it is possible to allow each of the phrases to say something very important and to allow our own prayers to develop from them. For example, in the phrase 'Christ be with me', we might well picture Jesus standing at our side in whatever situation we happen to be in at that particular moment of time. With the words 'Christ within me', we might imagine ourselves breathing the Holy Spirit into our bodies. 'Christ behind me' is an opportunity to reflect on the past day, on its good times and on its bad times, on the people and the events that have made it what it has turned out to be. Similarly, the words 'Christ before me' are an opportunity to think about the day that lies ahead, the opportunities that it affords and the people we will meet. 'Christ beside me' again brings the mind back to the present time with the reminder that Christ is actually here with us now, and the words 'Christ to win me' focuses the attention on the fact that it is actually him that is being served, and him that we are fighting for in our lives. The words 'Christ to comfort and restore me' are words to reflect on if there has been anything in the past day that has left us feeling hurt or bruised, or even if the past day has left us feeling very tired. With these words we can picture Jesus mentally, comforting us in a physical way, restoring and breathing his life-giving spirit into our pains. In any Christian's life there are bound to be things which cause anxiety and worry, and so we say 'Christ beneath me' as a support in any difficult times that lie ahead, and 'Christ above me' as a shield from harm and danger. Saying the words 'Christ in quiet, Christ in danger' can remind us of Christ's presence throughout the day, in times of joy and peace or times of fear and anxiety. The prayer then gives the opportunity to pray for those close to us in the words 'Christ in hearts of all that love me'; we can mention them by name, asking him to be with them as we picture him being with us. Finally the prayer ends with 'Christ in mouth of friend and stranger', asking for the wisdom to see Christ in others and for ears to listen to him speaking to us through them. If this prayer is prayed slowly and if time is taken to make the prayer more personal by adding inter-cessions and petitions as seem appropriate, then it can be a beautiful way of focusing our attentions and thoughts upon Jesus. There are many other prayers that can be used in the same way. The prayer 'God be in my head' is a beautiful way of starting the day in dedication to Christ.

God be in my head, and in my understanding.
God be in my eyes, and in my looking.
God be in my mouth, and in my speaking.
God be in my heart, and in my thinking.
God be at my end, and at my departing.

By far the most important and well-known prayer is the Lord's Prayer. Many people would be forgiven for think-ing that there is a magic formula attached to it since it is recited on so very many occasions. Selwyn Hughes com-ments on this practice:

Some Christians think that prayer consists solely of reciting the words of the Lord's Prayer, but, as the great preacher C.H. Spurgeon once said, 'To recite the Lord's Prayer and believe that you have then prayed is the height of foolishness'. This does not mean, of course, that there is no spiritual value in reciting it, provided

that we realise that it is not just a prayer to be recited . . .
but I do want to encourage them to view it as a depar-
ture point rather than an arrival platform.[6]

There are many commentaries available on the subject
and content of the Lord's Prayer, and it is well to be
familiar with some of these so that instead of just reciting it
quickly we can enter into it, and benefit in the fullest way
possible from the words that the Christian Church has
taken to be the central pivot and focus of its prayer life.

There are also many books of prayers available and they
can all be used in one of two ways. Either they can be
prayed as they are read, or else they can be used as
springboards to launch us into new dimensions of com-
munication with God. What Thomas Merton wrote about
a book of meditations could be just as true of a book of
prayers:

The purpose of a book of meditations is to teach you
how to think and not to do your thinking for you. Consequently if you pick up such a book and simply read it
through, you are wasting your time. As soon as any
thought stimulates your mind or your heart you can put
the book down because your meditation has begun.[7]

Using the Bible

Too often, prayer and the reading of the Bible are sepa-
rated when they should be bound together, and indeed
there are imaginative ways in which the one can help the
other.

Asking questions: It is wise to read small amounts of the
Bible at a time, for often it is true that the more that is
read, the less that is taken in. If the same amount of time
were taken to read a smaller portion of scripture, then it is
possible that more sense will be made of what is read.
Most modern translations of the Bible are printed with the
text subdivided into sections of around ten to twelve

48

verses. Rather than trying to read chapter upon chapter at any one time, it might be better to read just one of these smaller sections each day. Of course, one should not feel bound by this; some days the reading will go on for twenty or thirty verses, whereas other days there might be enough to cope with trying to understand two verses on their own. A pattern of reading may take the following form. The passage should be read and re-read so that it becomes familiar and time should be taken to ask certain questions about its content.

Who was this passage originally intended for?
What is the main purpose of this passage?
What does it tell us about God, or Jesus, or the Holy Spirit?
Does it reveal a sin that should be confessed?
Does it highlight a need or a concern that should be included in our prayers?
Does it bring to mind a person that should be prayed for, either in the form of intercession or in thankfulness?
Does it say anything about the way that we live our lives, or the way that we *should* live our lives?
Had we been in that situation, listening to those words, watching that action, what would our initial reaction have been?
Is God saying anything else to us through this passage?

By honestly answering these questions, thoughts are bound to emerge which will help in times of prayer. Let us examine in some detail how this might be done with this passage from Matthew:

You are the light of the world. A city on a hill cannot be hidden. Neither do people light a lamp and put it under a bowl. Instead they put it on its stand, and it gives light to everyone in the house. In the same way, let your light shine before men, that they may see your good deeds and praise your Father in heaven. (Matt. 5.14–16)

This passage could well reveal a failure on our part to witness to our faith, which is something that could be confessed, and as far as possible rectified in our lives. It may lead us to pray in general for the work of Christian witness and evangelism, or for the local ministers and their responsibility of spreading the good news. We might pray with thanksgiving for people who are bold enough to step out and be a light for the world, or for ourselves, that our lives may be a witness to others, and that God may highlight areas of our lives which are a stumbling block to others. By using this method, prayer is kept personal and we are saved from praying in such abstract ways as to render our prayers quite ineffectual.

Living the story: Another way of using the Bible to bring life to prayer is to meditate on a story until the reader becomes a part of what is going on. This method of meditation applies more to the Gospels than to other parts of the Bible. The first thing to do is to choose the passage and to read it until it becomes familiar. Let us imagine that our passage is Mark 11.15–17, the clearing of the temple.

> On reaching Jerusalem, Jesus entered the temple area and began driving out those who were buying and selling there. He overturned the tables of the money changers and the benches of those selling doves, and would not allow anyone to carry merchandise through the temple courts. And as he taught them, he said, 'Is it not written: "My house will be called a house of prayer for all nations"? But you have made it a "den of robbers".'

The point of this form of meditation is that the reader actually tries to put himself into the situation, in this case in the area of the temple, with all the noise and the smell of the animals. There are many pictures available of what the architecture may have looked like, and a brief study of this may help to make the meditation more lifelike. Once the scene has been set, we can imagine Jesus entering the temple, looking around, and beginning the work of clearing everything and everybody out of the area. We could then imagine ourselves to be in the temple area, surrounded by all the debris of the eviction that has just taken place, but alone with Jesus. We may feel at this point that there are areas of our own life that he would like to clear out, and so we could imagine ourselves talking to him and asking him what he would like to do, and hearing his reply.

A similar meditation could be based on one of the stories of Christ's healing miracles, for example the healing of blind Bartimaeus in Mark 10.46–52:

> As Jesus and his disciples, together with a large crowd, were leaving the city, a blind man, Bartimaeus (that is, the Son of Timaeus), was sitting by the roadside begging. When he heard that it was Jesus of Nazareth, he began to shout, 'Jesus, son of David, have mercy on me!'
>
> Many rebuked him and told him to be quiet, but he shouted all the more, 'Son of David, have mercy on me!'
>
> Jesus stopped and said, 'Call him'. So they called to the blind man, 'Cheer up! On your feet! He's calling you.' Throwing his cloak aside, he jumped to his feet and came to Jesus. 'What do you want me to do for you?' Jesus asked him. The blind man said, 'Rabbi, I want to see.' 'Go', said Jesus, 'your faith has healed you.' Immediately he received his sight and followed Jesus along the road.

In this instance we may imagine ourselves to be members of the large crowd that was following Jesus. What was it like to hear a voice cry out for mercy? Was there excitement when Jesus called over to him? What would have gone through our minds as we witnessed Bartimaeus seeing for the first time? How did Jesus react to the miracle that he had just performed? Finally, if we could have had a moment alone with Jesus after this great act had taken place, what would we have said to him? What would our answer be if he said to us 'What do you want me to do for you'?

By reading the New Testament, and especially the Gospels, in this way, it is possible to enter into the spirit of the works of Jesus perhaps as never before. It is possible to live the Gospels and to let them breathe their life into us, so that their words can become our prayers.

Tangible aids

So far, we have looked at ways in which written words, either in the form of the Bible or in set forms of Morning and Evening prayer, can be of use to anyone trying to put their thoughts into prayers. Aids to prayer, however, are not limited merely to the written word. There are several other symbols and objects that can be used to encourage prayer, and to aid the concentration. Concentration can be a major problem to many people when they are trying to pray. They want to pray, they have the will to pray, and indeed they have many things in their hearts which re- quire prayer — but this still may not be sufficient to hold their concentration. There is a sense in which that is not very important, for however feeble and full of wandering thoughts our prayers may be, the fact that one is trying to pray is enough. That might be true, but it does matter to *us* if it is difficult to concentrate on prayers. Hence there is sometimes the need for tangible aids to prayer to help focus the mind.

For some, a lighted candle may be useful. St Teresa of Avila once thought of God in these terms:

> . . . I conceive of my God as a brazier of burning coals, and if a small spark should be taken from it and fall upon the soul in such a way as to make it feel inflamed yet not consumed, it will continue in that pain which is so delightful.[8]

Jesus once said that he was the light of the world, and if this is so, then by placing a lighted candle in front of us we can be reminded, as St Teresa was reminded by the burning coals, that a small spark of the divine being is present with us. This does not mean that only a part of God is with us, for of course the full majesty of God goes with his servants, but there is in us enough to kindle within us a fire, burning brightly for our Lord.

Jesus probably spoke these words, 'I am the light of the world', at the climax of the Jewish Feast of Tabernacles, when a crowd would have been assembled, each person holding a lighted torch. In one part of the temple there would have been four large golden candlesticks, and by imagining the contrast between the darkness of the night and the brilliance of all the torches, our Lord's words, 'I am the light of the world', take on a new meaning. A lighted candle can do much to remind us of who it is that is being addressed and what his role is in the world. It is, of course not being suggested that prayers are being offered to the candle, but rather that the candle represents in a visual way what is invisibly present, namely the living God burning in our midst.

Having said this, it is worth mentioning that there are those for whom such a symbol will be of no use, and indeed it may serve as more of a distraction than an aid. If we find ourselves looking too much at the candle, or worrying about the dripping wax, then it is unlikely that it will be of much use in focusing our prayers and our attentions upon God. A symbol such as this should remain a servant, and if it ever becomes a master, then it is probably a good time to abandon it and try to pray without a symbol at all.

The candle is a reminder of who is receiving our prayers and a cross or a crucifix can serve a similar function. The beauty of the cross is that it needs no explanation as to what it is. It is an immediate pointer to the death and resurrection of Jesus. Just one glance at this symbol is a reminder of his love for us, and for those for whom we are praying. By the symbol of the cross, his commitment to us is re-emphasized and we are reminded of the extent to which he was prepared to go to demonstrate his love for mankind.

Another object that may be of some use is a picture or painting of one of the great gospel scenes. Throughout the ages, the Bible has always been a tremendous source of inspiration to all kinds of artists, and often the result of their labours has been given as much prayer as paint. Such pictures can still be of help to people in their prayers today. Most people have their own mental pictures of the accounts of Christ's ministry, and often it can give greater insight and understanding to see how others imagine these events. For example, a picture of one of the healing stories of the Gospels may lead us to ask certain questions about our own feelings and attitudes to the subject. By studying a picture for some time, we may feel that we can see ourselves within that picture, and it may lead us to a time of praise and thanksgiving for the power of Jesus, a time of confession for doubting his power. The reactions that are seen on the faces of the onlookers may lead us to ask what our own reaction would be to witnessing such an event. We might wonder which of the people in the picture we would identify with most — a Pharisee, a cripple, a disciple, or anybody else? Where a healing is depicted, we could also put into the picture the face of someone for whom we are praying, seeing them as the person that Jesus is touching.

There are those who find the smell of incense conducive to prayer, and often when people talk of an atmosphere that they like in church, they are referring to the lingering smell of incense. In the Old Testament, incense was used to accompany the sacrifices required by law, but elsewhere in the Bible, for example in Revelation 5.8, it is possible to see a symbolic link between incense and prayer:

. . . the four living creatures and the twenty-four elders fell down before the Lamb. Each one had a harp and they were holding golden bowls full of incense, which are the prayers of the saints.

If one chooses to pray surrounded by an atmosphere of incense, it can serve as a reminder of the prayers reaching up to the throne of God, and as a symbol of his presence with us — not that God is in the incense, but in the sense that just as one is constantly surrounded by the smell of incense, so one is also surrounded by the presence of God.

For many, prayer is purely a vocal exercise. By considering the use of aids such as the ones described above, it is possible to see that it is quite feasible to use many of the other senses in prayer as well, such as sight, touch and smell. In this way more and more of our body is allowed to participate in our prayer time. So often it is the case that we pray with our lips and all the other senses get in the way, providing distractions. However, as we have seen, they can be channels for prayer. Thus when we come to pray, our whole being can participate, and not just a small part of us.

Notes

1. Saint Teresa of Avila, *A Life of Prayer*, abridged and edited by James M. Houston, Pickering & Inglis, 1983, p. 2, section 10
2. William Law, *A Serious Call to a Devout and Holy Life*, SPCK, 1978, pp. 197–98
3. Kenneth Leech, *True Prayer*, Sheldon Press, 1980, p. 190
4. *Parish Prayers*, edited by Frank Colquhoun, from the Foreword by the Most Revd and Rt Hon. F.D. Coggan, Hodder & Stoughton Ltd, 1980
5. George Appleton, *The Practice of Prayer*, Mowbray, 1982, p. 75
6. Selwyn Hughes, *Every Day with Jesus*, CWR, July/August 1983, passage set for 2 July
7. Thomas Merton, *Seeds of Contemplation*, Anthony Clarke Books, 1972, p. 167

8. Saint Teresa of Avila, *A Life of Prayer*, abridged and edited by James M. Houston, Pickering & Inglis, 1983, p. 189

6. The calm and the storm

Sometimes it is quite amusing to listen to telephone conversations. For some it is just a normal conversation, but for others it can be a very one-sided affair, wherein one person takes the role of speaker and the other the role of listener. Much of the time the listener can do little except throw in a few 'ums' and 'ahs' just to show that he or she is still there.

There are those who treat prayer in the same way, always talking and never listening, always pouring out their hearts to God, but never receiving anything from him. There is, however, a solid Christian tradition of listening to God instead of always talking to him. Some make the mistake of thinking that being quiet before God means praying quietly under one's breath, but actually it is to do with being in a state of prayer without making any mental or vocal petitions. In his autobiography, Harry Williams speaks of a preacher whom he once heard:

> He took as his theme Samuel's prayer: 'Speak Lord, for thy servant heareth', and told us that too often our own prayers consisted of the opposite petition: 'Hear Lord, for thy servant speaketh.'[1]

Being quiet before God has many advantages. First, it can open the door for us to hear the voice of God in our lives; this can help us with the actual subject matter of our prayers as well as providing an opportunity for specific areas of guidance. Secondly, it can have an effect on the way we live. Too much time is spent hurrying from place to place, rushing through meals and skimming through our reading, thinking and praying, and many of us would benefit greatly from having a certain time to be at peace and allow the body to slow down and breathe in God's quietness. For those who would sacrifice that peace for the pursuit of knowledge and continuous activity, Thomas á Kempis said this:

> Firstly be peaceful yourself, and you will be able to bring peace to others. A man of peace does more good than a very learned man.[2]

Let us look at some practical ways in which this peace can be nurtured within us.

Being still

Being quiet requires great discipline; it requires a decision to shut oneself off from the rest of the world for a certain period of time. A separate time may have to be set aside for that purpose, for whereas it may be possible to make verbal and mental prayers on the bus or train, to be still and to be quiet means that all manner of distractions need to be guarded against and avoided. If possible then, it is best to be in a church, in the countryside or in a room where there will be no distractions, and where background noises can be kept to a minimum. However, now and again there are bound to be some disturbances and it is wise to make a decision in advance about how to deal with them. For example, the telephone may ring. Will I be able to ignore it or should I stop and answer it? Maybe it is possible to unplug the telephone during this time. If, for some reason, it is necessary to break off our prayers, it is better to go right back to the beginning and start all over again rather than try to pick up from where we left off, as any distraction is bound to leave us feeling a little breathless and disorientated.

The first stage involves relaxing the whole body. This is done by tensing and relaxing individual muscles and limbs, starting with the legs, until the whole body is relaxed and calm. It is important not to rush any part of this stage, as a few minutes spent in this way can be of enormous benefit in switching the mind from mental to silent prayer. The next stage is to quieten the spirit. The following method combines breathing and mentally reciting certain words.

First, empty the lungs of all air, and then slowly take a deep breath while saying the words, 'Come, Holy Spirit'. This should take about six or seven seconds. When the lungs are full of air, hold your breath for about the same length of time and say the words, 'Fill my heart'. Finally, again over the same period of time, slowly breathe out whilst saying, 'Cleanse me from all that offends'. Then repeat the whole process. Here is a resumé of that exercise:

Breathe in and say quietly:	'Come, Holy Spirit'
Hold your breath and say:	'Fill my heart'
Breathe out and say:	'Cleanse me from all that offends'

The natural temptation is to rush the entire procedure, but the slower this exercise is performed then the more beneficial it will be. Neither should we be in too much of a hurry to progress to the next stage; rather the process should be repeated over and over again, perhaps ten times or more, until we feel relaxed and ready to move on. One of the great joys of this method of stilling ourselves is that almost any words can be used so long as they are fairly rhythmical and divide evenly into three sections. Another set of phrases that is used by many people is: 'Lord Jesus Christ; Son of the Living God; Have mercy on me, a sinner'. It could be used in the same way as the previous example:

Breathe in and say:	'Lord Jesus Christ'
Hold your breath and say:	'Son of the Living God'
Breathe out and say:	'Have mercy upon me, a sinner'.

Still others find that the simple name 'Jesus' can have a profound effect on them as they repeat it over and over again, coupling it with a regular breathing exercise. An eastern monk, Father Lev Gillet, wrote this:

> In order to walk, one must take a first step; in order to swim, one must throw oneself into the water. It is the same with the invocation of the name. Begin to pronounce it with adoration and love. Cling to it. Repeat it. Do not think that you are invoking the name; think only of Jesus himself. Say his name slowly, softly and quietly. . . . In time you will find that the name of Jesus will spontaneously come to your lips and almost continually be present to your mind.[3]

For some this will come quite easily, but others may find that they have to practise over several weeks, and others still will not find it at all helpful. This does not matter for what is good for one person may be a complete distraction for somebody else.

Listening to God

We have now resolved to spend some time in silent prayer and practical steps have been taken to wind down the body, mind and spirit, so that we may now begin to listen in prayer to the voice of God. Let us look at some possible consequences of this resolution.

Asking God what to pray for

I know of one person who began to practise 'listening to God' in his prayer time and one day clearly saw in his mind the geographical outline of the Soviet Union. A few moments later he saw what seemed to him to be prison bars. Linking these two pictures together he began to pray for those suffering for their faith in that area of the world. The more he prayed for this subject, the more he felt troubled by it. As time went on he was able to find out the names of specific people in prison in Russia, and the more that he found out, then the more he was able to become prayerfully involved. Today that person sees that issue as his own specific topic of prayer, given to him by God, a topic that he wrestles with day and night. Many others could testify to a similar story. There is no way that we can force God to speak but by the practice of silence we can wait in hope for his voice in our hearts. Some claim to have actually heard a voice; for others it is more like a picture in their minds, while others still talk about an impression in their hearts, or words written across a screen in their minds. Whichever way it happens we can expect God to convey to us the subjects and the words for our prayers. Bishop George Appleton puts it this way:

> I have often been asked about the language in which God speaks. Some Jews with whom I have talked assert that He speaks in Hebrew. Muslims insist more strongly that He speaks in Arabic, the language of the Qu'ran. Cynical critics in the West suggest that He talks in English, with a growing American accent. My own belief is that He speaks in the language of the heart. This needs to be interpreted into thought and then expressed into words.[4]

Naturally this can take time. We cannot expect to close our eyes and immediately receive the abundance of God's wisdom — it may take a long while to empty our minds of our own thoughts and to wait in the silence for what may be forthcoming. It is not something that can be forced. Kenneth Leech says:

> We do not create prayer, but merely prepare the ground and clear away obstacles. Prayer is always a gift.[5]

Many people use mnemonics (key letters to aid the memory) to remind them of areas of prayer. One such mnemonic is SLOT, standing for Surrender, Listen, Obey, Trust. First all that is on our minds must be surrendered to God so as to be open to whatever he may wish to place there instead. The next step is to listen expectantly for God's word. A necessary part of surrendering and listening is that we do not assume that God will say only the things that we would say, or that we think he should say — there must always be room to be surprised by God. After this it is important to proceed to the next stage, that of obedience, and to obey the impressions received, and to pray as we feel directed. Finally we must trust that if God has spoken then he will honour his promise and fulfil his desires in his own time.

Seeking guidance from God

There is always a danger that what is believed to be the voice of God is none other than that of our own imagination, especially when seeking guidance about a particular decision we have to take. There are horrific stories about people who have sacrificed their position in society and gone out to foreign lands as missionaries, only to discover after a short while that they have made a great mistake, and what they assumed to be the voice of God in their prayers was nothing more than a projection of their own desires. Many times people ask God to reveal his will in their lives, but how can they be sure that what they hear is actually God's voice and not just their own? A distinct impression received whilst praying may seem to be a clear pointer for one's life, but how can that picture be tested? In other words, how is it possible to obey the biblical command to 'test the spirits'? Supposing that you had the clear idea that God wanted you to be a minister or priest. There is no major denomination that will take that as sufficient grounds for ordination. Everybody is subjected to a time when their vocation is tested, their conduct is examined, their prayer-life looked at and their overall suitability assessed. This also applies to anyone seeking to be a missionary with one of the major organizations. There must always be a time when vocation is tested. This passage is from Acts 13.2:

While they were worshipping the Lord and fasting, the Holy Spirit said, 'Set apart for me Barnabas and Saul for the work to which I have called them'. So after they had fasted and prayed, they placed their hands on them and sent them off.

Here we read that even after a direct word from the Holy Spirit there was no immediate action taken until after further prayer and fasting, presumably for the Spirit to confirm the word that had already been given. Only then were Barnabas and Saul finally commissioned by the rest of the church members. In the same way, we should have the wisdom to discuss with other Christians what we believe God is saying to us today. If it *is* the word of God in our hearts, then it will stand up to close scrutiny and will be none the weaker for having been tested in this way. If it is not, then we should be grateful for having had the opportunity to discover this, so that his real plan for us may be sought. If it is true that God does have a plan for each one of us, then it is important to discern the difference between his plan for us and our own wishful thinking.

The time that is set aside for our daily prayers should ideally be a combination of speaking to God and listening to him. There must always be the opportunity to share with our heavenly Father all that is in our hearts, but there must also be the opportunity to stand back in silence and allow God to minister to us.

Arrow prayers

If there is one category of people who perhaps find it more difficult to pray than any other it is mothers with babies or young children. Because of the demands on their time and the constant attention that they must give to their charges, having the opportunity to be alone and relaxed with God must seem like a dream. Are they ever able to pray? And for those who *are* able to set aside some time for God, what about the rest of the day? How can one continue to think about God during life's busy moments? In answer to both of these questions 'arrow prayers' or 'telegram prayers' can be quite helpful. An arrow prayer is simply a short prayer of one or two words that is silently or vocally directed up to heaven at appropriate moments. For most people, most arrow prayers are cries for help at specific times of the day, and there is nothing wrong in this. In *The Cloud of Unknowing*, the author describes how we shout out 'Fire!' or 'Help!' in an emergency and continues:

> Just as this little word stirs and pierces the ears of the hearers more quickly, so too does a little word of one syllable, when it is not merely spoken or thought, but expresses also the intention in the depth of our spirit. . . . And it pierces the ears of Almighty God more quickly than any long psalm churned out unthinkingly.[6]

There is no reason, however, why arrow prayers should just be limited to times of emergency. Far better for them to be used at every opportunity when prayer needs to be offered to God. First thing in the morning, for example, is a good time to dedicate oneself to God in preparation for the day ahead. George Stewart wrote:

> I would suggest that you write down a short form of such dedication . . . 'Lord of my life and God of my salvation, I offer this day to Thee. I would seek in all things to do Thy will, and use its hours as Thou wilt guide.' I suggest the use of some form prepared by yourself, so that morning by morning you do not need to think of words in which to express yourself, but saying the familiar words slowly and deliberately you can send your will travelling along these familiar lines.[7]

Who has not been overawed by the beauty of nature? Then is the time to offer arrow prayers of praise to God for the marvellous things that we see all around us, either in the home, in the street, or elsewhere. Arrow prayers of thanksgiving can also be offered when someone makes us happy or when we are able to bring a feeling of joy to someone else. In the same way, when something goes wrong or when we hurt others or offend them, or suspect that we have offended God, then our arrows should be those of confession to him. *The Cloud of Unknowing* also speaks of arrow prayers in times of spiritual dryness:

> Take a short word . . . A word like 'God' or 'Love' . . . and fix this word fast to your heart, so that it is always there come what may. It will be your shield and spear in peace and war alike. With this word you will hammer the cloud and the darkness above you.[8]

George Appleton also spoke of using a form of arrow prayer at times when he felt weary:

> Another practice which I have found helpful in a busy life as a diocesan bishop was when pressed or hurried or tired to claim the promise in our Lord's words 'Come unto me all that labour and are heavy laden, and I will refresh you', taking two or three minutes off, relaxing in a comfortable chair, and opening my whole being to his renewing strength.[9]

When the news is broadcast on the radio or television there is the chance to send an arrow prayer for those in need and ask for God's blessing upon them. By waiting until one's usual prayer time for this the chances are that the names and the details will have been long forgotten. Whenever we are out walking there is the opportunity to pray for those in the houses that we pass — some of them may be known by name and their situations can be lifted to God as we pass by. We can at the same time practise a form of meditation, thinking of how Jesus would react to the people that cross our path. George Stewart said:

> So again we may walk seeking to see the need of the streets. There will be needs that we cannot relieve, there will be needs that we could relieve easily but to which

we have been blind, and needs that we could relieve only at great cost. . . . As we walk we try to imagine what our Lord himself would have done in each case that our eyes fall on, and try to learn what He would have us do, and as we walk we ask God for His blessing on all.[10]

It is only a matter of practice before it becomes part of our routine to offer up such prayers. The point of arrow prayers is that they are not long and over-involved, but rather that the whole situation is placed into God's hand with a few short, well-chosen words. Perhaps one final use of arrow prayers is in dedicating activities to God before doing them. Many of us say grace before meals, so why do we not extend the practice to cover the whole range of our activities? G.K. Chesterton says:

> You say grace before meals,
> All right.
> But I say grace before the play and the opera,
> And grace before the concert and pantomime,
> And grace before I open a book,
> And grace before sketching, painting,
> Swimming, fencing, boxing, walking, playing, dancing,
> And grace before I dip the pen in the ink.[11]

If it is the case that arrow prayers are the only means available to offer up our feelings to God, then there is no reason why we should be excluded from enjoying a fulfilled and balanced prayer life. There is also no reason why any person's quiet time should not be enlarged and punctuated by the use of arrow prayers. We must take care, however, not to rely on arrow prayers too much and to let them become the only outlet for our prayers. If this becomes the case then, if possible, time should be set aside for prayers to be offered in a more formal setting and so that through the practice of silence a one-sided conversation with God can be avoided. Arrow prayers are better than no prayers at all, but ideally should be used to complement a more regular prayer time.

Notes

1. H. A. Williams, *Some Day I'll Find You*, Fount, 1984 (first published by Mitchell Beazley International), p. 211

2. Thomas á Kempis, *The Imitation of Christ*, translated by Leo Sherley-Price, Penguin Classics, 1983, p. 70

3. *Seasons of the Spirit*, Selected and edited by Every, Harries and Ware, SPCK, 1984, p. 105

4. George Appleton, *The Practice of Prayer*, Mowbray, 1982, p. 105

5. Kenneth Leech, *True Prayer*, Sheldon Press, 1980, p. 59

6. Anonymous, *The Cloud of Unknowing*, translated into modern English by Clifton Wolters, Penguin Classics, 1974, p. 97

7. George S. Stewart, *The Lower Levels of Prayer*, SCM, 1939, p. 131

8. Anonymous, *The Cloud of Unknowing*, p. 61

9. George Appleton, *The Practice of Prayer*, pp. 70–71

10. George S. Stewart, *The Lower Levels of Prayer*, p. 41

11. G.K. Chesterton, from his private notebook.

7. Praying with other people

There is really very little solitary prayer, for most vocal prayer is in connection with others. As we pray to God in our prayers, we become part of the whole worshipping community of Christians. One important part of confession is to correct our standing with our neighbours so that when we are in unity with each other, our worship may come from the heart as well as from the lips. Our intercessions are concerned with lifting up to God members of the community for him to pour his grace and healing upon them. As Neville Ward says:

> We are never allowed to forget that the body comes first and the members second. The pattern Christian prayer, the Lord's Prayer, is always said in the first person plural, even when we are alone, so that it is *we* who pray.[1]

It is only fitting that a book on prayer should have its final chapter on the subject of praying with other people.

Praying out loud

For many people, there can be nothing more terrifying than someone tapping them on the shoulder at the end of a prayer meeting and saying to them, 'Would you mind just closing in prayer?' Normally the truthful reaction to such a request is 'I'd really rather not!' though when put on the spot, most of us can manage to mumble a few words. The idea of praying aloud does however fill some people with absolute dread, normally because they have heard the prayers of others and feel quite unable to match them. It is well worth remembering that there are not many people who take easily to praying in public for the first time and most people know what it is to have a dry throat and a stammering tongue. Before looking at some of the occasions when we might be asked to pray aloud, let us look at some of the pitfalls to be avoided when praying in public.

First we should not remind people of the things that they have just heard which *we* might think need re-emphasizing. At the end of a meeting about financial responsibility, for example, we might be tempted to say, 'We thank you, Lord, for what we have heard tonight. May all of us, and especially those of us blessed with possessions, learn to be more generous with what God has given us.' Nor is prayer a time to advertise forthcoming meetings, 'We pray Lord, for the meeting of the Mothers' Union at 8.00 pm on Wednesday at 19 Browning Avenue — may you draw your people to it.' We should also be careful not to address God too confidentially. This can prevent others from participating because if the prayer is in such veiled terms that it is impossible for them to understand what is being prayed for, they cannot be sincere about saying the word 'Amen'.

Let us look at how to cope on some of the occasions when we might be asked to pray in public. There are some elements of prayer which are fitting on most occasions, such as a time of silence. This can give those present an opportunity to calm down and settle the mind and it also gives the person who is praying an opportunity to collect their thoughts. It is good to thank Jesus for his presence with the group at that time. Prayers offered at the beginning of a meeting have a dual task. They should commend to God the past day in order that everyone present can clear their minds in preparation for the meeting, and also ask for his blessing on what is about to take place. Saying the Lord's Prayer aloud together is especially useful in helping people to express their common purpose in coming together in Christ's name.

Prayers at the end of a meeting should contain elements of thanksgiving for the content or business covered. If the subject of the meeting was a guest speaker then it is good to pray for their ministry and witness. It is also in order to pray for those who have longer journeys to get home, and any future events in the days ahead. If the meeting has been a difficult one with a few raised tempers, then the job is more difficult. In prayer the aim should be to reach a feeling of oneness despite some temporarily broken relationships. A time for silence and an opportunity to shed our grievances and burdens upon God can help in circumstances like this. Closing with the Grace helps to close on a positive note.

There may be times when we are asked to lead the intercessions in church with little or no warning. Many orders of service give guidelines on how such prayers could be structured, but if no service book is available it is a good idea to have a plan to resort to in cases of emergency. Intercessions can often be the most difficult form of praying aloud because we are only too aware of the enormous quantity to be prayed for; and yet if the prayers are too detailed it may well be the last time that we are asked to lead the intercessions! One helpful way of constructing our prayers is to picture them reaching out in ever widening circles. Let us suppose that the setting is a small service of worship in a house. The gathering of those present would form the smallest circle, so the prayers could begin with petition for them, their families and friends, and their work. A slightly wider circle would include the church from which the members of that group come and prayers could then be offered for that church, its ministers, congregation and its work in the local community. So the prayer circles widen. The next may reach out to the local community itself and any socially-based community projects. A wider circle still would include the whole nation. People who lead prayers should be careful not to allow their own political colours to dominate, but on the other hand, if they feel strongly about an area of national concern, then of course, this should be mentioned. After our nation the widest circle of all is the world, and here topical issues can be raised. People can be positively helped in their prayers if they know that they are following some logical progression, and short periods of silence between each of the 'circles' of concern can distinguish between them and provide an opportunity for personal petitions to be added, either aloud or silently. In this way the 'Amen' at the end can be said with conviction by all present because they will have had a chance to follow the intercessor's train of thought without feeling that they have been bombarded with all manner of unrelated requests.

Prayer is a great privilege, and praying out loud is a great witness to that privilege. Often we are so afraid of making a fool of ourselves that we do not take the opportunity when it is presented. However, with practice it becomes easier and we can begin to feel less self-conscious. Perhaps the best time to practise praying aloud is at prayer meetings when time is given for people to contribute their own prayers. All that is required is a short prayer of a fairly specific nature. It is surprising how often these prayers confirm what someone else at the meeting is thinking. However shallow our efforts they can be used to glorify God and relieve the needs of our neighbours.

Praying as a couple

There is a story about a husband and wife, both committed Christians, who were very zealous in their individual prayer times, but they never prayed as a couple because neither of them realized that the other was, in fact, praying. Every evening the husband would make some excuse to nip off to the garage to tidy up, and there he would say his prayers; at the same time the wife would mutter something about going into the kitchen to make a cup of tea, and there she would say her prayers. Only one day when they were prevented from going about their normal routines did they discover the motives behind each other's behaviour and so, from that day, to their great joy, they began to pray together. It is a fact that those who have decided to share their lives on an intimate level as husband and wife sometimes find it difficult to share with one another in prayer. Indeed it can be a difficult thing to do if it has not been done before. There are various ways these difficulties can be overcome.

One method is that the couple could just sit in the same room and say their prayers silently and individually to themselves. This is a good beginning as it creates an awareness of praying together without the initial embarrassment that can accompany praying aloud for the first time. They could then progress to praying aloud together when they felt the time was right.

Another method is to follow set forms of prayer, such as the Church of England Morning and Evening Prayer. The versicles and responses could be said alternately, the psalm by alternate verses and the canticles said together. One person could be responsible for the readings and the other for the final prayers, which could be followed from the service book or made as spontaneous as he or she feels able.

After a time the couple may feel that they wish to make their prayer time more relaxed and spontaneous and may abandon set forms of prayer altogether and conduct their prayers in a time of free intercession and praise. Naturally none of these suggestions is limited to a husband and wife praying together, but are suited to any couple who wish to experience the joy of joining their voice with the voice of another in prayer.

One of the joys of praying with another person is being able to provide mutual support and encouragement by praying for each other. Another advantage is that when we become weary of offering the same prayers over a period of time, our prayer partner can bring freshness to our intercessions by praying from a different viewpoint and using different words.

Praying as part of a prayer group

When a group of Christians decide to pray together there is potential for a great deal of excitement as faith is shared and as expectancy in God arises. Sadly however, the joy can soon disappear from such occasions if the meetings become stale and dry, and the participants begin to go along more out of duty than out of a desire to meet together to pray. The key to maintaining interest lies in choosing carefully what, or whom, to pray for, and how to pray for them. So it is worthwhile spending some time at the beginning of the session thinking about the content of the meeting.

It may sound simple for a group to decide to pray for those areas in the world stricken by famine, but after some time such a subject can seem far removed from the comfortable group sitting in their arm chairs. However, if someone were to ask 'What do we mean when we pray for famine relief?', then this would provide an opportunity for the whole issue to be taken a step further. Questions need to be asked: Did God want the famine? How was it caused? What about the bereaved, the bitterness and the workers there? This applies to any topic that may be raised in prayer meetings. We may want to pray for the church — but what exactly are we praying for? Surely it is much easier to break down such a large subject into smaller sections, such as the clergy, the Sunday School, midweek groups and so on.

One way that the group could really function *as a group* when praying for a chosen topic, is to break down the subject into smaller issues as suggested above, and each member could then take away with them for that week one of these smaller issues and make it their own particular prayer concern under the umbrella of the wider subject that the group felt needed prayer. He or she could pray for that topic daily until the group met the next time, and then topics could be swopped so that different people could add fresh insight to a subject. In this way, it is possible to support prayerfully a needy situation over a long period of time without anyone feeling burdened by a concern that seems too big to cope with.

Through such discussion and real concern, the prayers of the group can be made more fervent and effective.

Getting the most out of church services

It is not unusual for two people to go to the same church service and for one of them to find it an uplifting and inspiring experience, and the other to come away feeling as if it was a complete waste of time. So how can we go into a church service with an attitude of mind that ensures that we will get the best out of this time? When Christians gather for worship, they do so as individuals coming together to be a corporate body. Ideally, this time of worship should be the climax of a Christian's week of prayer and study, and the launching pad into a new week which lies ahead. It makes sense, then, that we should be well prepared for this occasion. This can be achieved in various ways.

First of all, before going to church it is a good idea to read through the Sunday lessons if they are printed or advertised in advance. We could use one of the methods of using the Bible in prayer suggested in Chapter Five. In this way, when the lessons are read we will not be in the position of hearing them for the first time but rather will be reminded of familiar words. This may also help our appreciation of the sermon if it is based on the readings, since some of the difficult phrases and ideas will already have been grasped.

We can also prepare in advance for the moment of confession. The services do not include a time for lengthy reflection and self-examination, so the actual confession itself can fall short of our needs. We should be aware beforehand of our sins that need forgiveness so that the general confession can be a prayer of real repentance. So it can be useful to spend some time before church thinking over the past few days and remembering the actions and thoughts that have grieved God, others and ourselves.

There are also ways in which the time of intercession can be made more meaningful to us. At the end of the prayers the congregation are required to say the word 'Amen', which means 'So be it', in order to show common consent. If we are to be sincere in saying 'Amen', then it follows that as far as possible we should know those being prayed for and if they are sick should enquire about their progress and on occasions visit them. When world affairs are mentioned it is easier to say 'Amen' if we know a little about the situations mentioned and every effort should be made to keep up with the news, so that real fervency can be added to our individual prayers and those of the church.

Finally, we can pray for the actual service that is to take place, for the ministers, the preacher, the person leading the prayers, for the choir and any others who will be taking part, that they may perform their duties well and to the best of their ability, and that the Holy Spirit may use them to reach others.

After preparing for the service, we are ready for the worship itself. If we attend services regularly, it is amazing how much can easily be taken for granted. Week by week sermons are preached and very soon afterwards they have been forgotten. Yet the sermon can be one of the chief sources of growth for many people. It may be an idea to take a pen and paper to church to make notes on it so that afterwards the message can be studied and evaluated, and perhaps discussed with the preacher. In this way, the sermon can become a more interesting part of the service as it becomes not so much a monologue, but more of a dialogue, as we respond to what has been said and try to hear God speaking to us through the preacher.

Another part of the service that is often taken for granted is the actual Holy Communion itself, especially where there is frequent celebration of this event. Most of us who attend a communion service regularly would agree that it is a vital part of our lives, but because we have become used to what is going on, we can often take part without really being aware of what is happening. In *The Imitation of Christ*, Thomas á Kempis speaks of such a problem:

> If this most holy sacrament were celebrated in one place only, and were offered by one priest only in the whole world, men would rush to this place and to the priest of God, to be present at the divine mysteries. But there are now many priests, and in many places Christ is offered, that the grace and love of God may be better known to men, the more widely Holy Communion is diffused through the world.[2]

As far as possible, we should seek to approach the Communion as something special and unique, however many celebrations we may attend. It is important not just to read the words but to ask ourselves: What do we mean by these words? What is being signified by these actions? What are we promising to do?

Finally, after the service, there are three ways in which the meaning of the event can be extended into our lives. Some parts of the service, or some of the words spoken, will inevitably make more of an impression on us than others. These should be reflected on. As has been suggested, if there were points in the sermon that raised questions in our minds, a note could be made of them and they could be discussed with the preacher if he lives locally. Finally we should continue to pray for those mentioned in the intercessions, visiting the sick and, if possible, praying with them, and for those we have met and talked with in church, remembering especially those in any particular kind of need. In this way we can become a community of caring Christians, eager to learn more about our faith and attending church will be our focal point rather than merely an obligation to be fulfilled on one day of the week.

Services on the television and the radio

For many, listening to services broadcast on the television or radio is the only opportunity they have to worship with other people, and as with ordinary church services, it is quite possible to find very different reactions to the same piece of broadcasting. To some extent this is due to how much one is able to put into it, and it must be realized that watching or listening to a service needs a different approach from watching a film or a play. How is it possible to be an active participant in something that is being broadcast from many miles away? Let us look at this from two viewpoints, that of the presenters and of the listeners.

What are the presenters doing?

First of all they are *not* worshipping on our behalf. We hope they are worshipping in a way that includes, and not excludes, us. Their prayers are not pieces of literature that are meant to impress or call for critical appreciation; they are trying to create springboards to help us jump into the field of prayer itself. In other words, the aim of religious broadcasting is to sow seeds in the hearts of the listeners that these seeds may grow to the point where the listener is able to respond, not to the presenter, but to God. It can be seen in terms of building a tower to God: the presenter builds the foundations enabling the listener to build the walls.

The second thing that the presenter is not aiming to do is to please every person who may be listening or watching. Richard Harries recalls the advice he was given at the start of his broadcasting days:

There is an old woman sitting in a chair beside you. You've got your arm round her and you are talking to her — that's what you should be doing in broadcasting.[3]

The aim of the presenters then is not to speak to a crowd, imagining them all to be assembled just outside the studio; rather it is to imagine one person, you, and to give all they have to you.

What can we do?

Having looked at the aims of those who are presenting a broadcast, the most helpful point of contact would be if we could meet these aims. Our attitude is of primary importance. To listen to a service of worship with the attitude that it is something to be seen or listened to is the wrong way to start; better surely, if our attitude is that it is something that can be participated in and shared. On a practical level it may be helpful to imagine that instead of being a service that is broadcast, it is actually a prayer meeting in which the listener plays an active part. We can listen to the words, join in with the music, pray with the prayers, and in this way reach up to God in fellowship with others in the isolation of our own front room. It may be the case that there are several friends who are able to get together to widen the fellowship even further. In this way we do not need to imagine that we are part of a prayer meeting since the meeting already exists by virtue of likeminded people joining together.

The other aim of broadcasting that the listener can meet, and this applies more to radio than it does to television, is that of believing that the presenter is speaking to us individually. But for a leap of the imagination there is not really anything that can help this. Only by closing our eyes and hearing the words speaking to our hearts is it possible to feel that it is we who are being addressed and we who are being encouraged to pray and worship God.

Notes

1. J. Neville Ward, *The Use of Praying*, Epworth, 1968, p. 14
2. Thomas á Kempis, *The Imitation of Christ*, translated by Leo Sherley-Price, Penguin Classics, 1983, p. 187
3. *Kairos*, Easter 1984, No. 9

Acknowledgements

The author wishes to express his thanks to the following for permission to reproduce material of which they are the authors, publishers or copyright holders.

Avila, Carmelite Centre of Spirituality, for two extracts from *Saint Teresa on Prayer* by Jerome Lantry, OCD.

Baker Book House, Michigan, USA, for an extract from *The Hour that Changes the World* by Dick Eastman.

The Saint Andrew Press for extracts from *The Gospel of Luke* and *The Gospel of Mark*, both by William Barclay.

Anthony Clarke Books for extracts from *Seeds of Contemplation* by Thomas Merton.

Collins Publishers for extracts from *Prayers for Pagans and Hypocrites* by Peter De Rosa.

CWR for an extract from *Every day with Jesus* by Selwyn Hughes.

Epworth Press for extracts from *The Use of Praying* by J. Neville Ward.

Hodder & Stoughton Limited for extracts from *Prison to Praise* by Merlin R. Carothers, *Anything you ask* by Colin Urquhart, and the Foreword by the Most Revd and Rt Hon. F.D. Coggan of *Parish Prayers*, edited by Frank Colquhoun.

The Editor of *Kairos* theological journal for an extract from an article by Richard Harries in the Easter 1984 issue.

Mrs Howard Lindsay and Mrs Russel Crouse, New York, for an extract from the book of the musical *The Sound of Music*.

Mitchell Beazley Publishers for two extracts from *Some day I'll find you* by H.A. Williams.

A.R. Mowbray & Co. Ltd for extracts from *The Practice of Prayer* by George Appleton and *Turning to Prayer* by Richard Harries.

SCM Press Ltd for extracts from *The Lower Levels of Prayer* by George S. Stewart.

Sheldon Press for extracts from *True Prayer* by Kenneth Leech.

The Society for Promoting Christian Knowledge for extracts from *Seasons of the Spirit*, ed. Every, Harries and Ware, and from *A Serious Call to a Devout and Holy Life* by William Law (Classics of Western Spirituality series).

Henry E. Walter Ltd for extracts from *My Path of Prayer*, ed. David Hanes.

Paulist Press, New Jersey, USA, for US rights to reproduce extracts from *A Serious Call to a Devout and Holy Life* by William Law.

A.P. Watt Ltd, Literary Agents, on behalf of Miss D.E. Collins, for an eight-line poem from the private notebook of G.K. Chesterton.